From **AI desko** to **Zorbing**

From **Al desko** to **Zorbing**

New Words for the 21st Century

KERRY MAXWELL

Macmillan

First published 2006 by Macmillan
an imprint of Pan Macmillan Ltd
Pan Macmillan, 20 New Wharf Road, London N1 9RR
Basingstoke and Oxford
Associated companies throughout the world
www.panmacmillan.com

ISBN-13: 978-0-230-01468-8
ISBN-10: 0-230-01468-2

9 8 7 6 5 4 3 2 1

A CIP catalogue record for this book is available from
the British Library.

Designed by Rafi Romaya
Printed by Mackays of Chatham, Chatham, Kent

To Tom and Sam

Acknowledgements

I've been encouraged by many people in the writing of this book, but above all I would like to thank Guy Jackson and Kati Süle of Macmillan Education, without whose help and inspiration the book would not have been possible.

My thanks also to Penny Price, editor at Pan Macmillan, who has overseen the project with constant enthusiasm and efficiency. Also to Julie Crisp for her editorial assistance, to the book's designer, Rafi Romaya, and to Jean Maund for her excellent proofreading.

And finally I would like to thank my family and the many friends and colleagues who have helped and encouraged me in my work over a number of years, especially my partner Chris, whom I can always rely on for support and inspiration.

Grammar Guide

noun	book, teacher, truth
verb	make, arrive, be
adjective	happy, large, important
phrasal verb	give up, wear out
idiom	make ends meet, take the plunge

[C]	countable noun, a noun which is used with *a/an*, and has a plural form: *an apple, a teacher, examples*
[U]	uncountable noun, a noun which is not used with *a/an*, and does not have a plural form: *milk, health, advice*
[C/U] [U/C]	a noun which can be countable or uncountable: *a happy **marriage**, related by **marriage***
[plural]	plural noun, a noun which is always used in a plural form: *scissors, trousers*

[T]	a transitive verb, a verb which must have an object: *He **made** <u>a cake.</u>*
[I]	an intransitive verb, a verb which does not have an object: *She **arrived**.*
[I/T]	a verb which can be transitive or intransitive: *He **explained** <u>the</u> <u>problem</u>. Wait, and I'll **explain**.*
[usually passive]	a verb which usually appears in the passive form: *abbreviate*, e.g.: *'Thomas' **is** often **abbreviated** to 'Tom'.*

Pronunciation Guide

This book uses the following symbols for the pronunciation of words.

Consonants

p	b	t	d	ʃ
pen	**b**e	**t**ime	**d**ay	**sh**ine
f	v	θ	ð	ʒ
fast	**v**ote	**th**in	**th**is	mea**s**ure
s	z	tʃ	dʒ	x
sit	**z**ebra	**ch**air	**j**am	lo**ch**
m	n	ŋ	k	g
me	**n**o	si**ng**	**c**an	**g**ap
l	r	h	w	j
love	**r**ing	**h**ot	**w**e	**y**ou

Vowels and Diphthongs

iː	ɪ	i	ʊ	uː
s**ee**	**it**	prett**y**	b**oo**k	tw**o**
e	ə	ɜː	ɔː	u
egg	**a**bout	g**ir**l	c**au**ght	cas**u**al
æ	ʌ	ɑː	ɒ	aʊ
b**a**d	**u**p	**a**sk	**o**n	n**ow**
ɪə	eɪ	aɪ	ɔɪ	ʊə
h**ear**	s**ay**	m**y**	b**oy**	s**ure**
əʊ	eə			
g**o**	h**air**			

Stress

The main stressed syllable is shown by the symbol /ˈ/, and the second most important stressed syllable is shown by the symbol /ˌ/.

Normal Rapid Speech

Pronunciations of words often change in normal rapid speech. The schwa /ə/ often disappears between certain consonants and the sounds /d/ and /t/ can often not be heard when they are found between two other consonants. If these sounds are given in brackets, it means that they are often not pronounced by fluent speakers of English.

Introduction

The English language is a dynamic phenomenon. Like your mobile phone or the grass in your back garden, it is continually changing, shrinking and growing back again, constantly acquiring new characteristics. Many of these changes occur as a direct response to the way we live. As the world changes, we need to find different ways of describing it, to fill the gaps in our vocabulary for new concepts, and to ditch those words that refer to ideas no longer relevant to us. For instance, the word *video* is now yesterday's news, and the term *DVD* is well on its way to replacing it, just as not long ago the *compact disc* replaced the humble *record*. The word *Chunnel* has practically disappeared from use now the Channel tunnel has become a reality, but we've needed to introduce a distinction between *dial-up* and *broadband*, and the meaning of the word *web*, once just the home of a spider, has now been eclipsed by a computer-based information network.

At the time of writing (summer 2006), language experts are predicting that English is about to reach a significant milestone in its 1500-year history: the creation of its one-millionth word. Though the precise number of words in English will always be debatable, there is no doubt that it is a language of global importance with a vocabulary which is changing all the time. With the advent of the World Wide Web, both written and spoken English has a bigger platform for usage and propagation than ever before, and the words featured in this book are a testimony to this.

People often think that a word is only a 'proper', bona fide part of the vocabulary when it appears in a published dictionary. In reality, dictionary editors are pretty choosy about which new words they will include in new editions. To be included in a published dictionary, a word usually has to prove its worth over several years and across a range of different sources. Occasionally a word bursts onto the scene and seems likely to last, forcing lexicographers to sit up and notice. A recent (some might say unfortunate) example included in this book is the word *chav*, which made it into print within about a year of its first appearance. However, such cases are unusual, so that there are many words in regular use which haven't yet made the editorial grade. Only a handful of the words included in this book have so far made it into published dictionaries, but the rest are no less 'real' words whose longevity will not just be determined by lexicographers, but by the society in which they are used. Words stay in our language only if they represent concepts which continue to exist over the passage of time.

The really fascinating thing is that we, you and me, not a group of prescriptivists, academics or publishers, are the people who invent new words and embed them in the English language. And the processes we use to do this are not entirely random. Only a tiny fraction of incoming English words are shiny, brand-spanking 'new'. The majority of new words cleverly exploit the building blocks already present in English, using regular patterns of creativity.

One of the commonest mechanisms for describing something new is simply to combine two words, which together make a sensible representation of a new idea. Just as *text message* and *mobile phone* are now commonplace, the same creative process underlies many of the expressions in this book – compare *fat tax*, *voice lift*, *cuddle party* and many more. Sometimes the two words are fused together, so we get examples like *furkid*. Many others take inspiration from existing combinations, so from *fast food* we get *slow food*, and from *lifespan* we get *healthspan*.

Equally common is the combination, not just of whole words, but of *parts* of words, Consider *brunch* for example, which is a combination of the words *breakfast* and *lunch*. In the same way, we continue to take great pleasure in cannibalizing existing words and squeezing them together to make catchy items of new vocabulary. Some of the many examples included here are *flexitarian* (*flexible* and *vegetarian*), *podcast* (*iPod* and *broadcast*), *irritainment* (*irritating* and *entertainment*) and *movieokie* (*movie* and *karaoke*).

Sometimes we take the simple option of using a prefix which everyone recognizes and sticking it in a new place, so the book features examples such as *regift* (compare 're-' in *rewind*, *reinvent*, etc), and *miswant* (compare 'mis-' in *miscalculate*, *misjudge* etc.)

Abbreviations, especially those that function as acronyms, often form catchy additions to our vocabulary – remember 1980's *DINKYs*? (Referring to young, upwardly mobile professionals, and standing for ***d**ouble **i**ncome **n**o **k**ids **y**et.*) Some 21st century offerings featured here are *ASBO*, *BOGOF* and *SKI-er*.

Of course even easier than combining words is simply to find new ways of using words that already exist. Consider the new meanings of words like *window*, *mouse*, *virus*, *surf* and *net*, which are now part of everyday English. Following the same trend, examples in this book include *baguette*, *breadcrumb*, *rendition* and *zombie*, all of which have taken on new meanings in the 21st century. We also continue to follow the age-old tradition of simply nabbing words from other languages and using them as we see fit. Examples featured here include *tsunami*, *galactico* and *sudoku*.

So there it is. These are the main processes we use, often subconsciously, to change and expand our language. It remains to be seen whether the words themselves will last, whether a hundred years on people will go *speed dating*, become *flexitarians* or *SKI-ers*, *regift* their unwanted presents, and spend time doing a *sudoku*. But the processes underlying the formation of these words are more enduring, and will undoubtedly spawn the creation of many more new expressions in years to come.

abibliophobia

/ˌeɪbɪbliəˈfəʊbiə/ noun [U]

If you were camping in a remote mountain pass, would you start to panic as you turned over the last page of the only book in your rucksack? If so, that makes you a sufferer of **abibliophobia**, the fear of running out of things to read. And the cure for **abibliophobes**? – a visit to the nearest Internet café to browse the World Wide Web, an unlimited supply of reading material.

'You know summer is in full swing when the rapidly diminishing pile of books to read gives you a case of **abibliophobia** . . .'

(*NWOutdoorgrrl.com*, 4th August 2004)

afterparty also after-party, after party

/ˈɑːftəˌpɑːti/ noun [C]

After dancing the night away in a noisy and crowded nightclub, what better way to chill out than at an **afterparty**? In the comfort of an agreed venue, you can spend the early hours of the morning relaxing, chatting freely and consolidating any promising friendships that began during the main party. If you're lucky you might even get breakfast ...

'"Masterclass" captures the essence of a perfect night out, where outstanding music is an essential ingredient . . . each Masterclass release will take you on a journey from packed club dancefloor to early-hours **afterparty**.'

(*beatfactor.net*, 20th April 2006)

al desko

/ælˈdeskəʊ/ adverb, adjective

Do you have crumbs all over your computer keyboard as you read the news, do a bit of shopping, check the train times or book a holiday on the internet? Whatever happened to the time when our lunch break was a welcome excuse to leave the office and picnic in the fresh air? In the 21st century there are so many more reasons to eat **al desko** (whilst sitting at your desk) rather than *alfresco*.

'. . . a quarter of British workers are believed to have their lunch "**al desko**", often eating a pre-packed chain store sandwich in front of their computers.'

(The *Derby Gripe*, 22nd August 2005)

alcolock

/ˈælkəʊˌlɒk/ noun [C]

Before you put the key in your car ignition, stop. Now was that large glass of red wine you just drank one unit of alcohol or two? If you're not sure, then what you need is an **alcolock**. Through the wonders of modern technology, the **alcolock** can check your identity and monitor your alcohol levels as you breathe into the steering wheel, and if you're over the limit, the car won't start. Let's hope you can afford a taxi!

'A trial of **alcolocks**, initially in the Midlands and Bristol, will test whether people using them are less likely to drink and drive . . .'

(*Observer*, 29th February 2004)

ambush marketing

/ˌæmbʊʃ ˈmɑːkɪtɪŋ/ noun [U]

Imagine throwing a party where you've invited lots of interesting people and made a huge effort to provide lovely food and drinks. Imagine your partner had absolutely no involvement in planning or funding the party, but then waltzes in at the last minute and claims all the credit. Sounds unfair, but this is the essence of **ambush marketing** – when one product brand pays to become a sponsor of a large-scale event, and a competing brand connects itself with the same event without paying the fee.

'Piles of "bootleg" water bottles have started to gather outside the gates of the All England Club in southwest London after security guards at Wimbledon thwarted an **ambush marketing** attempt by Colgate-Palmolive.'

(*Times Online*, 29th June 2005)

Asbo also ASBO

/'æzbəʊ/ noun [C] British

One of the more controversial acronyms of the 21st century, **Asbo** stands for *Anti-social behaviour order*, a civil order intended to deal with those individuals who persistently make life unpleasant for others, usually through drunken behaviour, abusive language, vandalism, etc. Unruly nine year olds should watch their step too, as there's a version created especially for them, the **Basbo** (*baby Asbo*).

'I am at a loss to understand the concern over the implementation of **Asbos** . . . Why is it wrong for someone who persistently and wilfully behaves to the distress of others to be sent to prison?'

(*Guardian*, 30th December 2004)

awareness bracelet also **awareness band**

/əˈweənəs ˌbreɪslət/, /əˈweənəs ˌbænd/   noun [C]

Who would have thought that a mass-produced silicone rubber wristband would become one of the must-have fashion accessories of the noughties? You too could join the ranks of David Beckham, Nelson Mandela and Bono, and promote worthwhile causes by buying an **awareness bracelet**. Remember though to choose the right colour: blue for anti-bullying, pink for breast cancer, black and white for racism …

'The white anti-poverty wristbands . . . are not the first of the so-called **awareness bracelets** to generate a frenzy so great that would-be wearers are prepared to pay inflated prices to get their hands on — and in — one.'

(*Guardian*, 11th February 2005)

babyccino also **babycino**

/ˌbeɪbiˈtʃiːnəʊ/ noun [C]

If parenthood is cramping your coffee-drinking
style as your offspring plays with the sugar bowl at
your favourite café, why not introduce your little
one to the delights of a **babyccino**? Apparently a
cup of milky froth topped with a spoonful of
chocolate powder will keep an infant entertained
long enough for Mum or Dad to drink and chat at a
leisurely pace – and hopefully buy another cup or
two.

'It is just a cup of milky froth but the
babycino has become one of the crucial factors
in the battle to win the hearts of Sydney's
coffee drinkers.'

(*Sydney Morning Herald*, November 6th 2005)

baby hunger

/ˈbeɪbi ˌhʌŋgə/ noun [U]

If you've sacrificed the joys of parenthood for professional success, beware of the grip of **baby hunger** as your biological clock starts to tick more loudly. This overwhelming desire to hear the patter of tiny feet is mostly observed in professional women over the age of thirty, who in their **baby-hungry** state can prey on unsuspecting males and trap them in the web of fatherhood.

'Male **baby hunger** is not as great as women's — few have to make such a stark choice between reproduction and professional success. Baby peckishness, perhaps.'

(*Observer*, 28th April 2002)

babymoon

/ˈbeɪbiˌmuːn/ noun [C]

You're a twosome about to become a threesome.
Before the cycle of round-the-clock feeding and
endless nappy changing begins, why not get away
from it all on a **babymoon**, your last chance to have
a romantic, carefree, just-the-two-of-you vacation?
Parents-to-be who love to travel see a **babymoon**
as the final opportunity to relax in far-flung
locations before adjusting to the new reality of
pushchairs, baby food and sleepless nights.

'**Babymoon** getaways let parents-to-be have a
bundle of fun before bundle of joy.'

(*The Philadelphia Inquirer*, 16th April 2006)

baguette

/bæˈget/ noun [C]

There was a time when if someone asked you where they could buy a **baguette**, you would immediately point them in the direction of the local bakers. In the 21st century, however, you might also legitimately direct them to the nearest department store, since as well as being a long crusty loaf, a **baguette** is now also a slim wide handbag with a short strap.

'Strolling along with a Fendi **baguette** bag under her arm, every self-respecting Parisian or Milanese girl sends out a clear message: class, good taste, high buying power.'

(*Café Babel*, 3rd April 2006)

barbecue-stopper

/ˈbɑːbɪkjuː ˌstɒpə/ noun [C] Australian

Not a sudden downpour of rain as the sausages
start sizzling (this is Australia, not Britain), but a
topic of conversation that's so controversial it's
likely to call a halt to barbecue preparations.
A **barbecue stopper** can also be a social gaffe, an
embarrassing mistake which is so awkward that it
temporarily suspends conversation and burger
consumption.

'The issue of children's obesity has been one
of the **barbecue-stoppers** of the last political
year, with some people saying our kids need to
do more sport, and others saying they need
less fast food and sugary drinks.'

(*ABC Online*, 6th September 2004)

barista

/bəˈrɪstə/ noun [C]

As you order your next latte or cappuccino, spare a thought for the poor tired feet of the **barista**, that person behind the counter at your local coffee bar who churns out copious amounts of hot, steaming espresso, battling through requests for *skinnys*, *mochas, americanos* …

'In a warehouse choked with enough *eau de caffeine* to make a slumbering panda leap up and tap dance, two dozen of this region's finest **baristas** — aka those hip folks manning your local coffee bar — are grinding, frothing and plotting their way toward nothing less than global supremacy.'

(*USA Today*, 19th February 2003)

big up

/ˌbɪg ˈʌp/ phrasal verb [T]

You'd really been looking forward to seeing that film. Your friend had raved about it, and as soon as it was out on DVD you rushed out and got it. But then, after two hours slumped on the sofa, what a disappointment – it wasn't half as good as you expected. Whoever told you about it must have really been **bigging** it **up**!

'Mark Todd was a finalist in the first series, but his experience of MasterChef is less of a dream come true . . . "They **bigged** it **up** as life changing — it wasn't [for me]."'

(*BBC.co.uk*, 26th April 2006)

bird flu

/ˈbɜːd ˌfluː/ noun [U]

Beware of a highly contagious form of flu which has sent shockwaves throughout the 21st century world, responsible for hundreds of human deaths and the culling of millions of birds across the globe. Characteristics in humans range from colds and flu-like symptoms, such as coughs, sore throats and muscle pain, through to viral pneumonia and other major respiratory complications.

'The world must prepare for a long-term fight against **bird flu** and not give in to fatigue that seems to have set in, a senior World Health Organization (WHO) official warned.'

(*Reuters*, 26th April 2006)

BlackBerry (also **Blackberry**) **thumb**

/ˌblækb(ə)ri ˈθʌm/ noun [U]

Nothing to do with stained fingers after picking at bramble bushes, but the latest in repetitive strain injuries. If like many other owners of a *BlackBerry*™ handheld device, you send as many as 500 e-mails a day, then be careful, you could start to suffer from **BlackBerry thumb**. Spare a thought for your poor old thumbs and their daily workout through all that electronic communication.

'Medical science has not yet found a cure for that scourge of the Internet age — **BlackBerry Thumb**, the hand soreness that results from thumb-typing on personal digital assistants such as the BlackBerry mobile e-mail device.'

(*San Jose Mercury News*, 3rd April 2006)

blamestorming

/ˈbleɪmˌstɔːmɪŋ/ noun [U]

Your project was a failure and has spoilt the department's record of achievement. But just whose idea was it anyway, and why did things go wrong? Call a meeting to discuss it, and instead of *brainstorming*, why not try **blamestorming** – that way you can show that you had nothing to do with it!

'Back in the eighties and early nineties, everyone was talking about brainstorming, but more often than not what actually went on was **blamestorming** — people sitting in meetings, allegedly to share ideas but really saying "Who made the mistake?" . . .'

(*Business Week*, 24th September 2004)

bling also bling-bling

/ˈblɪŋ/, /ˈblɪŋ ˈblɪŋ/ noun [U]

Going to a party? Why not add some sparkle to your looks and jazz up an old outfit with a bit of **bling**? What about a really **blingy** chunky gold bracelet? Or you could **bling up** that cheap dress with a diamond necklace and **blingtastic** earrings. And as you arrive at the party, you might even overhear someone saying: 'she's dressed up well **bling**'.

'Their players' boots could all turn into diamond-studded **bling** boots, which really bring out the sparkle in their eyes . . .'

(*Guardian*, 28th March 2006)

blog

/ˈblɒg/ noun [C], verb [I]

If you'd like to share your opinions with the entire world and sound off to your heart's content, start writing a **blog** (online journal) – there are no word limits in cyberspace. Become a **blogger**, and you can write endlessly about whatever takes your fancy, from politics and the state of the world through to next door's cat or the latest Jamie Oliver recipe.

'Why **blog**? . . . In the back of each **blogger's** mind lurks that desire for someone to look into a **blog** of theirs and find an intellectual, witty, interesting person . . .'

(*ProgressiveU.org*, 27th April 2006)

blook

/blʊk/ noun [C]

The printed page has been overthrown by electronic media, or has it? In a bizarre twist, *blogs* (online journals), are becoming **blooks**, texts made of real bits of paper that you can hold in your hand. If you've ever fancied writing a book, you could pay to have your *blog* printed and join the ranks of a growing number of bloggers who see themselves as budding authors of **blooks**.

'Julie Powell wrote a blog about her attempts to cook all the recipes in an old French cookery book. Her blog was turned into a **blook** and to date she's sold 100,000 copies. Now that's food for thought!'

(*DailyIndia.com*, 19th April 2006)

bluejacking

/ˈbluːdʒækɪŋ/ noun [U]

Feeling bored as you stand in a queue? Why not enjoy a spot of **bluejacking**? Take your Bluetooth™-enabled mobile phone from your pocket, and use its wireless technology to discretely send anonymous text messages to the people around you. Join the ranks of the **bluejackers**, and enjoy the startled faces of the recipients.

'"I came across the idea of **bluejacking** at an online discussion forum and it immediately struck me as a fun thing to do," . . . She said the "priceless" expression on the face of her first victim as he tried to work out what was going on has turned her into a regular **bluejacker**.'

(*BBCi News*, 4th November 2003)

body lift

/ˈbɒdi ˌlɪft/ noun [C]

Do you have around $7,500 to spare? Think twice before splashing out on a luxury holiday or a new kitchen. This amount of cash could buy a completely new you. Rather than just a *face lift*, treat yourself to a complete **body lift** – within a few hours your thighs, buttocks and stomach could be transformed!

'Mine was a seven-hour procedure,' Gretencord said of her lower **body lift** . . . 'He actually took about 10 pounds of skin. Then he did extensive liposuction down in my legs and back and stomach and thighs. I went from a size 14 to a size 8/10 . . .'

(*Akron Beacon Journal*, 28th March 2006)

BOGOF also **bogof**

/ˈbɒɡˌɒf/ noun [C/U], adjective

Not a rather impolite way of telling someone to go away, but an acronym for 'Buy-**O**ne-**G**et-**O**ne-**F**ree' and now commonplace in our supermarkets. **Bogof** promotions leap out at us as we push our trolley around the store. They're very difficult to resist, and often leave us wondering where exactly we're going to store those twelve extra toilet rolls and that second bag of oven chips …

'Welcome to a world where Buy One Get One Free (**BOGOF**) — be it soft drinks or juices or garments or your fav brand of deo or moisturiser — rules your psyche and your purse alike . . .'

(*Times of India*, 6th April 2006)

bookcrosser

/ˈbʊkˌkrɒsə/ noun [C]

If in a bored moment on a train, in a café or some other public place you gratefully pick up a book left there by someone else, then you could be indebted to a **bookcrosser**. You could even tell the world what you thought of the book by logging on to the **bookcrossing** website and joining the world's biggest reading group. Drop the same book in a coffee bar or train carriage and you've become a **bookcrosser** too.

'**Bookcrossers** release a previously read book "into the wild" then follow its travels on www.bookcrossing.com, communicating and connecting to others who cross its path.'

(*Savannah Morning News*, 12th May 2006)

bouncebackability also **bouncebackibility**

/ˌbaʊnsbækəˈbɪləti/ noun [U]

If things are not going so well for you at the moment, reassure those around you not to give up hope, because you've got what it takes: remind them of your **bouncebackability**. You may have lost every game this season or just failed your exams, but success may be just around the corner!

'We have been beaten, but we will never be defeated . . . I for one, am looking forward to next season as we will prove that we have **bouncebackability**.'

(*Holmesdale Online*, 19th May 2005)

breadcrumbs

/ˈbredˌkrʌmz/ noun [plural]

A new sense of **breadcrumbs** which is not remotely connected to a seasoned coating on chicken or fish. In the language of web design, **breadcrumbs** are a string of words which represent the path of pages a person has visited as they navigate their way through a website. Inspiration comes from the age-old fairy tale of Hansel and Gretel, who left a trail of breadcrumbs to help them find their way out of the forest.

'The **breadcrumbs** are a trail that helps people browsing the School of Education's Web pages to keep track of where they are in relationship to the Home Page . . .'

(Website of the *University of Birmingham*, 28th September 2001)

bromance

/ˈbrəʊˌmæns/ noun [C]

Dave has recently got to know Nick, a new guy at the office. The two get on like a house on fire, regularly enjoying a bite to eat at lunch time or a quick drink after work. It's the early stages of what promises to be a good friendship, or, in the 21st century, a **bromance**, a blend of *brother* and *romance* which, contrary to what you might think, indicates that Nick and Dave are not sexual partners, but just good mates.

'Aries, this is a great week to have a **bromance** with yourself. Be your own best pal, take yourself out for pizza . . .'

(*San Francisco Bay Guardian*, Vol. 40, No. 25, March 2006)

budgie smugglers

/ˈbʌdʒi ˌsmʌɡləz/ noun [plural] Australian

Any man planning a trip to Bondi beach should think carefully about his swimwear options. If he hasn't added a pair of loose-fitting swimming shorts to his wardrobe in recent years, and still favours those tight-fitting swimming briefs like the ones manufactured by *Speedo*™, then as he takes to the waves he'll be wearing a pair of **budgie smugglers**.

'Ashlee made it clear from the start she was impressed by Aussie men, when she appeared on stage surrounded by men wearing **budgie smugglers** . . .'

(*Sydney Morning Herald*, 16th April 2006)

bustitution

/ˌbʌstɪˈtjuːʃn/ noun [U/C]

You arrive at the station, exhausted after work, to discover that your train has been substituted by a bus. You get on the bus and join a group of unhappy, complaining people. You're another victim of **bustitution**, and as the bus drives slowly down the road, you know that your journey will take at least twice as long as usual …

'If we are serious about encouraging people in the long term to make journeys by rail, that will not be achieved by **bustitution** and branch line closures.'

(Jeremy Corbyn, transcript of House of Commons debate, 6th December 2004)

cage diving

/ˈkeɪdʒ ˌdaɪvɪŋ/ noun [U]

If a quick dip in the sea doesn't hold enough excitement for you, why not join a group of thrill-seeking tourists off the coast of South Africa and try a **cage diving** trip? You too could be lowered deep into the sea in a steel cage, and, as you clutch your underwater camera, become human bait in exchange for a tête-à-tête with a great white shark.

'. . . He has also gone **cage diving** off the coast of South Africa to see the Great Whites in action and declares it an "amazing" not life-threatening experience . . .'

(*Liverpool Daily Post*, 1st September 2005)

chad

/tʃæd/   noun [C/U]

Just a totally harmless piece of paper, but
responsible for a major controversy at a US
presidential election. Those tiny little **chads**, the bits
of paper that are supposed to pop out when a
voter punches their ballot slip, can render votes
indecipherable by not completely detaching
themselves. The pesky little chaps have proved
themselves so problematic that millions of dollars
have been spent developing **chadless** voting
systems.

'. . . despite tens of millions of dollars spent
after the Florida recount fiasco to update
American voting technology, **chad** is alive and
well – and just as threatening as ever.'

(*ABC News*, 11th September 2004)

chav

/tʃæv/ noun [C]

Thick gold neck chains and heavy bangles, white trainers, short skirts, (counterfeit) Burberry check, designer sportswear and baseball caps. The fashion hallmarks of the **chav**. Who would have thought that a social stereotype, a pejorative description of an 'underclass' of young men and women, would become a buzzword in the early 21st century and jump the queue for a place in the dictionary?

'Britain's Prince William celebrated passing his first year of Army training by becoming a working-class "chav" . . . The handsome prince donned a loose-fitting top, a baseball cap and heavy jewellery for his new look.'

(*Monsters and Critics.com*, 10th April 2006)

Chelsea tractor

/ˌtʃelsi ˈtræktə/ noun [C] British

A daily challenge as you pick up your kids from school: where to park your modest little Ford Fiesta, which you'll doubtless have to shoehorn into the limited street parking because every inch is occupied by large 4x4 vehicles with names like Defender, Explorer, Discovery and Shogun. Otherwise known as **Chelsea tractors**, these jumbo cars are a familiar sight in suburban streets and supermarket car parks.

'The sight of small children piling out of a gleaming 4x4 . . . at the end of the congested school run is a familiar one . . . Keeping **Chelsea tractors** away from schools will be just one element in an assault on "pushy parents" by the Association of Teachers and Lecturers . . .'

(*Observer*, 9th April 2006)

chocotherapy

/ˌtʃɒkəˈθerəpi/ noun [U]

If you're the sort of person who loves to get their chops around a big bar of choccy but wakes up the next day with a face covered in spots, **chocotherapy** could be just the thing for you. Lie back as therapists apply cocoa and cocoa butter to detoxify your skin, and breathe in that mouth-watering aroma without putting on an ounce in weight – the chocoholic's dream!

'. . . my chocolatey body was wrapped in plastic on a heated bed like a gigantic Quality Street on a radiator. Did I rush to the nearest shop with a massive chocolate craving when I left? Strangely, no. How brilliant to get all the pleasure of chocolate without the guilt of eating it . . . Gerard's 100% **Chocotherapy** . . .'

(*Guardian*, 13th August 2005)

chugger

/ˈtʃʌɡə/ noun [C]

The next time you see a smartly dressed person standing with a clipboard in the centre of a shopping mall, think twice before you try to avoid them. This person could be a *charity mugger*, or **chugger**. **Chuggers** aren't interested in where you shop or which toilet roll you use, they just want you to sign up for regular donations to charity.

'I was recently ambushed by a charity mugger, or "**chugger**", in Oxford Street, London. "Good morning, sir. Do you like children and would you like to help them?" . . .'

(*Guardian*, 11th January 2005)

citizen journalist

/ˌsɪtɪzn ˈdʒɜːnəlɪst/ noun [C]

Armed with a digital camera and weblog software, anyone has the tools to become a reporter. Well before professional camera crews and photo journalists arrive on the scene, ordinary people with video cameras and camera phones can provide instantaneous footage of events. These are the **citizen journalists**, people who use digital technology and web-based media to share what they witness with a worldwide audience.

'Journalism is undergoing tremendous change, with blogs and **citizen journalists** proliferating and news consumers having more control over what they read, hear and see.'

(*Washington Post*, 25th April 2006)

contrasexual

/ˌkɒntrəˈsekʃuəl/ noun [C], adjective

Thirty-something, single, desperate for a man, in search of love …? If this is definitely <u>not</u> you, then maybe you're a **contrasexual**. The antithesis of *Bridget Jones*, the **contrasexual** woman is super-confident, wants to have fun, and stay single. She's not remotely interested in finding 'Mr Right', and, as for motherhood, well, that's just an inconvenience which will jeopardize her career …

'BOYS, say hello to the **contrasexual** woman. She is more interested in a round-the-world adventure holiday than settling down and starting a family . . . If men believe all single women are like Bridget Jones — ditzy, insecure, obsessively counting calories and desperate for a man — they'd better think again.'

(*London Evening Standard*, 5th November 2004)

crackberry also CrackBerry

/'krækb(ə)ri/ noun [C]

If you break out in a cold sweat when you can't find your *BlackBerry*™ (wireless handheld device), if you have the desperate urge to check and send e-mails several times a minute, then maybe you're a **crackberry** addict. Like alcohol or drugs, you could be addicted to wireless communication, and always need to feel the comfort of the Internet in your inside pocket.

'The Blackberry, a portable phone that also receives e-mails, is taking over the lives of many American executives and not always for the better. Some executives have become so hooked that it is now known by some as the **crackberry**.'

(*Washington Times*, 23rd November 2004)

cuddle party

/ˈkʌdl ˌpɑːti/ noun [C]

If life isn't going too well at the moment and you desperately need someone to hug, why not seek some emotional comfort by going to a **cuddle party**? Pay the required fee, and you could help create feelings of well-being as you join the *puppy pile* (the group of cuddling participants). Be careful what you do though, because your behaviour will be carefully monitored by the *cuddle caddy*.

'. . . nearly all of us are desperate for someone, anyone, even someone we've just met, to hold us . . . our needs fulfilled, we might venture back into the real world, boasting that we'd been to a **cuddle party**, the grandest social experiment since the 1970s . . .'

(*Seattle Times*, 5th September 2004)

Cyber Monday

/ˈsaɪbə ˈmʌndeɪ/ noun [C/U] American

We've got Shrove Tuesday, Ash Wednesday, Maundy Thursday, and Good Friday, and now the US has **Cyber Monday**, which, not surprisingly, has nothing to do with Lent or Easter, but refers to the Monday after the US Thanksgiving holiday. The weekend after Thanksgiving is the biggest shopping weekend of the year in the US. Back at work on the Monday, it seems that people continue shopping in *cyber*space, resulting in a sudden surge in online purchases.

'**Cyber Monday**, the Monday after Thanksgiving, is quickly becoming one of the biggest online shopping days of the year.'

(*CNN*, 25th November 2005)

cyberchondriac

/ˌsaɪbəˈkɒndriæk/ noun [C]

You've been feeling unwell and your Doctor is
doing some tests. The results will take weeks, so a
mouse click here and a keystroke there and hey
presto, that's what the problem is, you've found a
website that tells you everything you need to
know. But, hang on a minute, you didn't realize that
you're likely to suffer coughing fits, internal
bleeding, severe abdominal pain, and probably
only have weeks to live … Before you know it,
you've become a **cyberchondriac**!

'Are you a **cyberchondriac**? Cyberchondria has
become the new epidemic of the internet age.
The condition occurs when people become
convinced they are gripped by a terrible
medical condition after "recognising" their
symptoms on the web.'

(*New Zealand Health News*, May 2006)

cyberslacking also cyberloafing

/ˈsaɪbəˌslækɪŋ/, /ˈsaɪbələʊfɪŋ/ noun [U]

Sitting at our desk in the office, it's no longer just a quick chat or phone call that breaks the monotony of a working day. The Internet now gives us a whole new opportunity to avoid work. Hidden in *cyber*space, it looks as if we are busily typing as we shop, e-mail friends, read the news, check the scores, or book a holiday – but watch out, you too could be caught **cyberslacking**!

'Everyone does it. Millions of people use their office internet access to check out cheap flights, home shopping or celebrity gossip. Sending e-mails . . . has become a common ritual in the working day, but now there's a new term for personal use of the corporate web server — **cyberslacking**.'

(*Scotsman*, 28th June 2003)

Delia effect also Delia power

/'diːliə ɪˈfekt/, /'diːliə ˌpaʊə/   noun [U]

When celebrity chef Delia Smith cooked a particular recipe on her TV programme, little did she know that, as well as causing a nationwide shortage of lemon zesters, she would establish a new phrase in English. As soon as a celebrity shows us something on the telly, it seems that we all have to rush out and buy it – the **Delia effect**. Though it all started with Delia, it's a phenomenon not confined to cookery programmes or Delia herself.

'Appearing on the daytime talk show has been akin to winning the lottery for new writers as [Oprah] Winfrey's endorsement has the **Delia effect** on novels . . .'

(*Guardian*, 8th April 2002)

dental spa

/'dentl ˌspɑː/ noun [C]

Forget the dentist's surgery with its intense lighting and sinister whirring of the drill. Take a trip to a **dental spa**, and enjoy the complete toothcare experience. Sit in the special vibrating chair under subdued lighting, and surf the net, watch TV, or have a foot massage. Relax and say 'aaah', and you'll hardly notice the maintenance of your pearly whites!

'Thousands of dentists splash subdued colors on their walls and light candles to enhance their offices . . . But a true **dental spa** incorporates spa treatments as well, such as massage therapy or another relaxation technique . . .'

(*Indianapolis Star*, 26th November 2004)

denture venturer

/ˌdentʃə ˈventʃərə/ noun [C]

If you've had a long working life and those last few years before retirement seem a depressing prospect, then why not join the ranks of the **denture venturers**? It's the 21st century, and a *gap year* (a year away from work in order to travel) isn't just for young student types, but for oldies too. Why not blow all your hard-earned savings on a pre-retirement trip around the world?

'. . . rising numbers of older people in the population of developed countries, together with the increased health and wealth of this age group, has helped to spawn pre-retirement gap travellers . . . an ever increasing number of 50–55 year olds are . . . becoming so-called "Denture Venturers".'

(*Scotsman*, 16th September 2005)

deshopper

/diːˈʃɒpə/ noun [C]

Ever bought something, used it a little bit, and returned it to get your money back? If so, you're a **deshopper**, and if we're totally honest, the majority of us will have done a bit of **deshopping** in one form or another. The most unscrupulous **deshoppers** will purchase things with the deliberate intention of using and returning them, like buying a DVD, watching or copying it, and returning it for a full refund.

'They buy a CD to copy it and return it to get their money back. They are the **deshoppers** — a scam that has cost stores £63 million this year.'

(*London Metro*, 8th December 2004)

digerati also digirati

/ˌdɪdʒəˈrɑːti/ noun [plural]

You might have heard of the *glitterati*, the rich and famous folks so often the focus of the media. Then there's the *chatterati*, those columnists, talk-show hosts, etc. who are constantly putting the world to rights. In the technology-driven noughties, we now also have the **digerati**, those technical experts who form the *cyber* elite, the most influential doers, thinkers and writers of the online universe, or at least they like to think they are …

'Its collapse symbolises the dashing of yet another dot.com dream for San Francisco's **digerati**, who enjoyed legendary rooftop parties at the magazine's headquarters to celebrate the thriving internet economy . . .'

(*Guardian*, 17th August 2001)

dirty bomb

/ˈdɜːti ˌbɒm/ noun [C]

First there were *conventional* weapons – knives, swords, guns and explosives. Then the 20th century gave us *unconventional* weapons, as the world became preoccupied with chemical and nuclear warheads. Now into the noughties we've gone one step further and decided it would be a good idea to combine both conventional and unconventional ways of harming people, and develop the **dirty bomb**, a device which uses conventional dynamite to disperse unconventional radioactive materials into the atmosphere.

'A radiation sensor inside a cell phone was used with a network of tiny computers spread out around Vanderbilt Stadium on Thursday to detect a fake radioactive **dirty bomb**.'

(*CBS News*, 21st April 2006)

dog-whistle politics

/ˌdɒg wɪsl ˈpɒlətɪks/ noun [U]

Not *sheep* as a metaphor, but a *sheep dog*. In sheep farming, a dog-whistle is used to create a special high-pitched sound which only attracts the attention of a particular dog, rather than all the dogs around. Think of the whistle as a political message, and the dogs as the voting public, and you get **dog-whistle politics**: present your message so that only your supporters 'hear' it properly – particularly useful if you are dealing with sensitive issues, like immigration perhaps …

'Thatcher's was true **dog-whistle politics**, a subtle signal rather than the main message.'

(*Observer*, 24th April 2005)

dooce

/duːs/ verb [T] (usually passive)

You've had a particularly bad day at the office and you need to relieve the tension by having a really good moan about everyone and everything. If you decide to write about your problems in your *blog* (online diary), then think again. If you say something which criticizes people you work with, without realizing it you could expose yourself to the possibility of being **dooced** (fired)!

'The rise of blogging has also brought an increase in the number of people being "**dooced**" — sacked for blogging about their company.'

(*New Zealand Herald*, 27th May 2005)

dotbam also **dot-bam, dot bam**

/ˌdɒt ˈbæm/ noun [C]

It's a tricky decision. Do I buy that new sofa by a simple click of a mouse button, sitting in the comfort of my own home sipping coffee, but run the risk that it might be the most uncomfortable seat I've ever purchased, or do I go to the store, battling my way through the crowds, but safe in the knowledge that I'll be able to give it a thorough test drive? Such is the dilemma presented by the **dotbam**, a high-street retailer who offers online shopping.

'Next came the newly revamped Thomas Cook website, which was praised for its reliability and "strong brand", making it the best of the **dotbams**.'

(*internettravelnews.com*, 14th May 2001)

dumb up

/ˌdʌm ˈʌp/ phrasal verb [T]

Your boss is never satisfied. First she asks you to *dumb down* the report because it shows too much technical detail and will be difficult for others to understand. The next thing you know, she's asking you to **dumb** it **up** by adding complex calculations to make it look more impressive.

'The new consumer trend of **dumbing up** is set to edge aside the celebrity-fuelled vacuity typified by the likes of *Closer*, Vicki Pollard and *Celebrity Big Brother* this year, according to a trends agency. DDB Signbank . . . has identified a desire for greater intellectual rigour as a key trend for 2006.'

(*Guardian*, 13th January 2006)

DWY

/diː dʌbljuː ˈwaɪ/ abbreviation

Mobile phone users beware. You may have heard of criminal offences like *DUI* (Driving Under the Influence) and *DWI* (Driving While Intoxicated). If you wouldn't dream of drinking and driving, but just can't resist picking up your phone (you dropped it on the passenger seat and now it's within easy reach and ringing enticingly), consider **DWY**, the 21st century crime of *Driving While Yakking* (into a phone).

'New York is about to become the first state to restrict the use of cell phones while driving but it won't be the last . . . There are 18 other states considering similar bills that prohibit people from driving while yakking (**DWY**) on their cell phones . . .'

(*Wired News*, 27th June 2001)

Dyson

/ˈdaɪsən/ verb [I/T], noun [C]

In his autobiography, vacuum cleaner entrepreneur James Dyson talks of his dream that: 'one day, Dyson will replace "Hoover" and become a noun, a verb, out there on its own, long after I am forgotten ...' Good news, Mr Dyson, because as the 21st century progresses, more and more of us, it seems, are **Dysoning** up the crumbs from the living room carpet, or tidying the bedroom and giving it a quick **Dyson** ...

'The penny dropped as I stood in my living room staring at a sooty pigeon that had wriggled down the chimney . . . as I **Dysoned-up** the feathers and pigeon poo, I realised I was doing it wrong.'

(*Guardian*, 1st October 2005)

earworm

/ˈɪəˌwɜːm/ noun [C]

We all know that feeling of hearing a catchy tune on the radio and then being bothered by it for the rest of the day. Now we've finally got a way to refer to it, instead of talking about 'this song which keeps going round and round in my head'. This is the **earworm**, invading our consciousness for several hours until it finally gets removed, often by another **earworm**!

'The company shifted its focus from background music to foreground; the music suddenly wanted to be noticed, to implant "**earworms**" — musical phrases you can't get out of your head — into the disc changer of your brain.'

(*Washington Post*, 19th June 2005)

Ee

edutain

/ˌedjʊˈteɪn/ verb [T]

Let me **edutain** you …You might have heard the adage that 'learning is fun', and that's what being **edutained** is all about. We can feel less guilty about our kids spending so much time glued to computer or TV screens if we think that what they're watching or playing is in some way educational. Television programmes, websites, computer and video games, all can be used to provide **edutainment**.

'An hour-long, audio program that helps parents stay sane by keeping 6–9 year olds **edutained** with acted-out stories, toe-tapping music, jokes, goofy characters and laughs . . .'

(advertisement, *cdbaby.com*, 2003)

ego-surfing also egosurfing

/ˈiːɡəʊˌsɜːfɪŋ/ noun [U]

Wouldn't it be great to discover that you were actually quite famous? If you do a spot of **ego-surfing** (looking for occurrences of your name on the World Wide Web) then you might make the surprise discovery that you're a minor celebrity in the virtual world! What's more likely, however, is that you'll discover there are quite a few other people in the world with the name: 'Andrew Blenkinsop'.

'You might think your name is unique, but an **ego-surfing** film-maker is here to prove you wrong . . . I was happy with my name until I found on the internet that I was one of at least 15 Vanessa Thorpes in Britain.'

(*Observer*, 14th January 2001)

elderweds

/'eldəˌwedz/ noun [plural]

It's never too late to tie the knot. If you're getting on a bit but have been lucky enough to meet someone you'd like to spend the rest of your years with, then why not join the ranks of the **elderweds** – people aged sixty or over who re-marry or marry for the first time? And if one or both of you have kids from previous relationships, you can all go on one, big, happy *familymoon*.

'Where earlier the word was newlyweds, today it is **elderweds**, to refer to all those people who get married later in life.'

(*Tribune, India*, 19th July 2003)

embed

/ɪmˈbed/ noun [C]

Embed is no longer just a verb, but a noun too.
During the 2003 war with Iraq, US military officials
and news organizations placed hundreds of
reporters, photographers and cameramen in
military units. These are now known as **embeds**,
professional journalists put in military units to
provide news coverage throughout a war. The noun
might be new, but the concept certainly isn't.
Before he rose to political greatness, Winston
Churchill was a war correspondent who got his first
break by becoming an **embed** during the Boer War.

'There are about 45 **embeds** in Iraq right now,
primarily the U.S. and U.K.'

(*townhall.com, Washington DC*, 8th April 2006)

eVest also **e-Vest, Scott eVest®**

/ˈiːvest/, /ˌskɒt ˈiːvest/ noun [C]

If you're the sort of person who can't quite manage a walk in the countryside without access to the gadgets of the noughties, then the **eVest** could be just the thing for you! An **eVest** is a waterproof jacket designed specifically to store all those gadgets you can't manage without. It has pockets which can accommodate your mobile phone, PDA, MP3 player or even laptop computer, with clever fabric channels which allow you to conceal wiring and route it up to your collar.

'We're the first to admit a little wariness nowadays towards any product with an "e" affixed to its surname, so when we learned of a jacket with an "e" in its title we were pretty skeptical. But we were pleasantly surprised with the new **Scott eVest** . . . The **eVest** has 10 pockets of varying size for every conceivable gadget you might need . . .'

(*PC Magazine*, June 2002)

extended financial family also EFF

/ɪkˌstendɪd faɪˌnænʃ(ə)l ˈfæm(ə)li/ noun [C] British

Rising property prices, interest rates, student debt,
escalating cost of residential care ... It's no wonder
that the wider family are needing to join forces to
buy a home. An **extended financial family** is a
group of three generations of the same family –
grandparents, parents and children – who live
under the same roof, simply because this makes
good financial sense.

'According to research by Skipton Building
Society, the UK is about to see a new
economic unit – **the extended financial family
(EFF)** – emerge as a major social trend over
the next twenty years.'

(*www.findaproperty.co.uk*, 29th April 2004)

extreme ironing also EI

/ɪkˌstriːm ˈaɪənɪŋ/ noun [C]

Most of us curb the boredom of wading through a pile of ironing by listening to the radio or watching TV, unaware that we're missing out on the thrills of a new extreme sport – **extreme ironing**. Armed with a cordless iron, ironing board and a few items of laundry, participants scale the heights of mountains, trek through forests, surf, ski, canoe, snowboard or do just about anything which enables them to iron in the most bizarre situation or location.

'**Extreme Ironing** devotees like nothing more than removing creases from their clothes halfway up cliffs, on top of mountains or in busy city streets . . .'

(*BBC News*, 7th August 2002)

fanfic also fan fic, fan fiction, fanfiction

/ˈfænˌfɪk/, /ˌfæn ˈfɪkʃn/ noun [U]

If you're so addicted to the adventures of *Harry Potter* and his chums that you cannot possibly wait until the next novel comes out, then why not bridge that gap by writing some stories yourself? You'd be joining lots of other budding authors in a new literary genre called **fan fiction** or **fanfic**, where fans write their own stories using the characters and settings from a series of books, films or TV programmes that they're mad about.

'Many popular shows inspire fans to create their own scenes and post them to community Web sites, a phenomenon referred to as **fanfic**.'

(*Reuters*, 23rd April 2006)

fat finger syndrome

/ˌfæt ˈfɪŋɡə ˌsɪndrəʊm/ noun [U]

Doing the supermarket shop online. Really convenient, but occasionally risky. Suddenly you're unpacking *sixteen* cans of baked beans, and as the penny drops, you realize you must have keyed the number four at the 'packs of four' option on the screen, rather than at the 400g can you usually have. The scenario of accidentally entering the wrong details into a computer is so much a part of everyday life that we now have a name for it: **fat finger syndrome**.

'The trader at Mizuho Securities . . . fell foul of what is known in financial circles as **fat finger syndrome**, where a dealer types incorrect details into his computer.'

(*The Times*, 9th December 2005)

fat tax

/ˈfæt ˌtæks/ noun [U/C]

As you put those Danish pastries, chocolate biscuits and jelly beans into your trolley, think how much more expensive your shopping bill would be if anything temptingly sweet and delicious were subject to a **fat tax**. Still, it only shows the government cares about your health, since you are currently more likely to die from heart disease than cancer …

'A Downing Street-based policy unit has proposed a plan to place a **fat tax** on junk food in an attempt to tackle the rising incidence of heart disease . . .'

(*Telegraph*, 19th February 2004)

flash mob

/'flæʃ ˌmɒb/ noun [C]

If you're stuck for something to do this weekend, why not join a hundred other people and stand in a big huddle outside your local shopping centre? Through the wonders of online communication, you could find out if there is a **flash mob** gathering near you. **Flash mobbers** are a large group of people who, just for the fun of it, suddenly get together in a public place, do something for a short time, and go away again.

'London has its first taste of the **flash mob** phenomenon, with a spontaneous crowd turning up at a sofa store.'

(*BBC News*, 8th August 2003)

flexitarian

/ˌfleksəˈteəriən/ noun [C]

A culinary dilemma – you've got your friend coming round to dinner who's a strict vegetarian, and also your parents-in-law who will doubtless be expecting some kind of roast beast. How much easier life would be if your friend were a **flexitarian**, prepared to eat a little meat or fish for the evening just to make life simpler for you …

'**Flexitarians** adhere mostly to the vegetarian diet as a healthy lifestyle rather than following an ideology. They feel an occasional meal that includes fish, fowl or meat is acceptable.'

(*Los Angeles Times*, 8th June 2004)

flirtberrying

/ˈflɜːtˌberiɪŋ/ noun [C]

It's the 21st century and on Valentine's day you don't even need to buy a card, just pick up your mobile phone and send an instant message to the one you luuuurve. If you're lucky enough to own a *Blackberry*™, with its text messaging, e-mail and wireless Internet facilities, then you have the ultimate gadget for expressing romantic interest whilst on the move. Why not get 'fruity' with your *Blackberry*™ and go **flirtberrying**?

'. . . I believe that February 14 is about sending strange messages to people you hardly know . . . Talking of strange messages, BlackBerrys have been all over the news. I contacted the makers and was told by their PR people of a phenomenon called **flirtberrying**, sending flirty e-mails with the device.'

(*The Times*, 12th February 2005)

flyboarding also fly-boarding

/ˈflaɪbɔːdɪŋ/ noun [U]

If you're really happy with your home and have absolutely no intention of moving for at least another twenty years, imagine waking up one morning to discover that a 'Sold' sign had mysteriously appeared outside your house? What a shock – but a likely explanation is that you've become another victim of **flyboarding**, where estate agents put 'For Sale' or 'Sold' signs outside properties which are not for sale as a cheeky way of drumming up publicity.

'Two London estate agents have been fined more than £18,000 for littering the streets with bogus to-let boards. Andrew Chard and Barry Manners, directors of Chard Estate Agents, pleaded guilty at West London magistrates' court to eight offences of **flyboarding**.'

(*Evening Standard*, 11th November 2005)

folksonomy

/fəʊkˈsɒnəmi/ noun [C/U]

There are literally billions of items of information on the Internet, and the prospect of categorizing them all is a humongous task. But there's a simple solution – why not get web users to do it themselves? Users can add their own keywords to particular websites as a way of categorizing the information that they find there. If enough of them do this, patterns begin to emerge, and the result is a **folksonomy**, an online classification scheme generated by us 'folk'.

'**Folksonomies** are bottom-up classifications which lack rigour . . . but may well resonate better with users — and in any event represent the only feasible way of tagging content on the web.'

(*Observer*, 27th November 2005)

free running

/ˌfriː ˈrʌnɪŋ/ noun [U]

If a quick jog around the park just doesn't hold enough excitement for you, have you ever thought about taking up **free running**? For **free runners**, the urban landscape is one gigantic playground. They treat man-made structures as an obstacle course, vaulting over bollards and benches, scaling lamp-posts, flipping over road barriers, climbing high buildings and leaping between rooftops in a death-defying way. Now that should get the adrenalin pumping!

'Such was the exhilaration packed into . . . this dazzling film about **free running**, you may well have spent this morning eyeing up bollards and calculating the speed and trajectory required to get from the roof of your office to the fire escape of the building opposite.'

(*Guardian*, 10th September 2003)

freegan

/ˈfriːgən/ noun [C]

Have you ever seen unopened packages of food on a restaurant table or in a rubbish container and thought 'What a waste – someone could have eaten that!'? If so, maybe you should consider becoming a **freegan**. With a more relaxed attitude to 'use by' and 'best before' dates, you could adopt environmentally friendly principles and live for *free* off the waste of a consumer-oriented society.

'Vegan for two years, she became a vegetarian at age 9 and was "**freegan**" for a while. For her, this meant not paying for meat or animal products but eating them if they were left over or destined for the trash . . .'

(*Seattle Weekly*, 8–14th June 2005)

furkid also **fur kid, fur-kid**

/ˈfɜːkɪd/ noun [C]

If looking after a baby seems like too much hard work, why not think about getting a **furkid**? You could hear the 'patter of tiny paws' rather than the 'patter of tiny feet', and your new furry companion, whether it's a dog, cat, or guinea pig, wouldn't just be a pet, but a substitute offspring. You could lavish all your parenting impulses on it, safe in the knowledge that it won't answer you back or eventually want to drive your car!

'Couples like **furkids** because they usually don't live long enough to need expensive private schools. And their friends like **furkids** because, unlike real children, you can plausibly claim to be allergic to them.'

(*ABC Network, Australia*, 2004)

galactico

/gəˈlæktɪkəʊ/ noun [C]

Recently earning itself a place in the dictionary,
galactico has nothing to do with astronomy or a
particular brand of chocolate bar, but in fact refers
to a famous, very highly paid professional
footballer, typified by the likes of Brazil's Ronaldo
and England's very own David Beckham. Based on
the same word in Spanish which means 'superstar',
a **galactico** is strategically purchased to improve
the performance of a team – but does he always
deliver the goods?

'Germany skipper Michael Ballack was today
unveiled as the latest Chelsea **galactico** as the
Premiership champions underlined their
intention to retain the title for a third time
next season.'

(*Mirror*, 15th May 2006)

Gg

garbology

/ˌgaːˈbɒlədʒi/ noun [U]

The next time you go out to your rubbish bin, consider how what you're going to throw away might reveal a little something about the life that you lead. The majority of us dispose of a wide range of food items and domestic products every day, which when accumulated might reveal something about our habits. **Garbology** is the analysis of this idiosyncratic combination of refuse, and **garbologists** are people who study other people's trash.

'AFTER the crowd has long gone at the famous English racecourse, shadowy figures are sifting through the rubbish left behind . . . A strange sight, perhaps, but this is known as **garbology** . . .'

(*The Sunday Times*, 11th June 2006)

geolocation

/ˌdʒiːəʊləʊˈkeɪʃn/ noun [U]

There was a time when, as we sat at the computer innocently surfing the net or doing a bit of online shopping, we felt anonymous in the virtual world, no one knowing who we were or where in the world we happened to be. Thanks to the technology of **geolocation**, however, Big Brother could indeed be watching you – or at least know where you are. Online criminals beware – banks can now find out exactly where you're sitting as you conduct those fraudulent transactions!

'Prominent among those tools is **geolocation**, the web geography technology that determines the true geographic location of the online customer at the moment he clicks into the website — the country, state or even city.'

(*BankersOnline.com*, 25th April 2005)

globesity

/ɡləʊˈbiːsəti/ noun [U]

As you tuck into the turkey, mince pies and all those other Christmas indulgences this year, remember that you could be affected by one of the major health risks of the 21st century, the worldwide epidemic of **globesity**. The World Health Organization has suggested that the widespread problem of obesity, especially in the developed nations, represents a more serious health risk than smoking. It is estimated that by the year 2017, 75 per cent of British men and women will be overweight!

'**Globesity** gains ground as leading killer . . . It's a bitter truth to swallow: About every fourth person on Earth is too fat. Obesity is fast becoming one of the world's leading reasons why people die.'

(*Associated Press*, 10th May 2004)

Google also **google**

/'guːgl/ verb [I/T]

Doing a *Google*™ search on the Internet, now one of the utensils of everyday life, much like making a telephone call or using the vacuum cleaner. So much so that, just like *hoover* before it, *Google*™ has now had the honour of becoming a verb. Arguably one of the most effective and powerful search engines on the web, we favour it so much that its name is now synonymous with 'to search for something on the Internet'.

'I **Googled** my name in a period of boredom the other day. I was amazed at the number of times it came up on the Internet search.'

(*Columbia Daily Tribune*, 7th May 2006)

Googlewhacking

/ˈguːɡlˌwækɪŋ/ noun [U]

Forget the daily crossword, it's the age of the Internet, and puzzle fanatics have a new diversion, **Googlewhacking**. Believe it or not, **Googlewhackers** while away the hours looking for combinations of words which give exactly one single result when entered into the *Google*™ search engine. Their ultimate goal is to see the words 'Results 1–1 of 1' appear on the screen, and with the billions of web pages indexed by *Google*™, this represents a real challenge!

'What do "bathetic weasels", "gusseted hobbits" and "zoroastrian chipmunks" have in common? . . . they are examples of a craze that has taken the Internet by storm . . . **Googlewhacking** . . . has become a pastime for everyone from bored office workers to lexicographers and even Nasa scientists.'

(*Observer*, 26th October 2003)

googolplex

/ˈguːɡɒlˌpleks/   number, verb [I/T]

Imagine a number so big that to write it down would need a supply of paper bigger than the known universe! This is **googolplex**, which is the number ten, raised to the power ten, in turn raised to the power one hundred. **Googolplex** is an inconceivably large, but not infinite number. It is sometimes used as a verb, 'to googolplex', which means 'to increase by an unimaginably large amount'.

'Since we introduced the pocket numbers game into the United Kingdom in November, it has **googolplexed** into a national craze and international pandemic.'

(*The Times*, 14th May 2005)

grafedia

/grəˈfiːdiə/ noun [U]

What if the Internet were all around you, extending beyond computers and wireless connections, and expanding down city streets, appearing on lamp-posts and the sides of buildings, going into restaurants and popping up on wine bottles, beer mats and even tattoos? This is the aim of **grafedia**, underlined bits of text written, chalked and spray-painted in public places. Though they may look like *graffiti*, they actually function as electronic addresses which give access to Internet-based media.

'This is the vision behind an interactive new media project called **grafedia**, which enables folks to make the world their canvas by publicly posting e-mail addresses or keywords that, when punched into certain mobile phones or an e-mail account, retrieve corresponding images.'

(*Wired News*, 25th March 2005)

greenwash also green-wash

/ˈɡriːnwɒʃ/ verb [T] (often passive)

Have you ever bought an organic, environmentally-friendly shampoo, only to discover that in fact it contains chemicals such as 'sodium lauryl sulphate' and 'propylene glycol'? If so, you have been **greenwashed**! From advertising designed to convince people of eco-friendliness, through to government policies alleged to promote the well-being of the environment, **greenwashing** is common practice in the 21st century.

'Professor John Whitelegg, the Green party spokesman on sustainable development, commented: "If HSBC, Shell and BP need a man to **greenwash** their appalling environmental record, then Blair is certainly the man for the job."'

(*Guardian*, 27th April 2004)

grief tourist

/ˈɡriːf ˌtʊərɪst/ noun [C]

A visit to the grave of a person you didn't know wouldn't instinctively be a number one holiday outing. Well, maybe not for you, but it seems that a new breed of **grief tourists** are interested in just such an activity. Specially arranged coaches transport visitors to the scene of a tragedy. People flock in their thousands to the memorial of a celebrity they felt they 'knew' …

'. . . the phenomenon of conspicuous compassion reached a "fearsome" peak in August 2002 when thousands of "**grief tourists**" descended on the Cambridgeshire town of Soham to leave flowers and cuddly toys in memory of the murdered schoolgirls Holly Wells and Jessica Chapman.'

(*Telegraph*, 23rd February 2004)

gripesite also gripe site

/ˈɡraɪpˌsaɪt/ noun [C]

If you feel that you've had a raw deal as a consumer, and you want to protect others from the same fate, the Internet provides you with the golden opportunity to tell the whole story and put the record straight. Launch a **gripesite**, and you can spell out the facts about faulty goods or deficient services to a potentially worldwide audience.

'Quick-tempered Americans really lose it when they've been had as consumers. Increasingly, they are taking out their anger on strongly worded Internet **gripe sites**.'

(*USA Today*, 7th February 2005)

guerrilla gardener

/gəˌrɪlə ˈgɑːdnə/ noun [C]

You're walking past some wasteland one day, and suddenly you notice shrubs and bedding plants poking out of the soil. That's strange, you think to yourself, you walked the same route yesterday and you could swear they weren't there then … It looks like **guerrilla gardeners** have been at work, gathering with their garden spades in the depths of the night to surreptitiously enhance the urban landscape.

'**Guerrilla gardeners** are sowing the seeds of resistance in south London, with a spot of illicit gardening in its neglected public spaces.'

(*BBC News*, 21st March 2006)

half-birthday also half birthday

/ˈhɑːf ˌbɜːθdeɪ/, /ˌhɑːf ˈbɜːθdeɪ/ noun [C]

Do you need an excuse for a celebration, because Christmas and your birthday are still a few months away? Or maybe your birthday falls on a really annoying date, like Christmas Eve or February 29th? If so, then why not follow *Harry Potter*'s example and think about celebrating your **half-birthday** – the day that falls exactly six calendar months either before or after your real date of birth.

'It's happy **half birthday** to the first of 76 million baby boomers who turned 59½ on Friday and can take money out of their retirement accounts without paying a 10 percent early-withdrawal penalty . . .'

(*Sun Herald*, 3rd July 2005)

hand-me-up

/ˈhænd miː ˌʌp/ noun [C]

Maybe as a child you had to suffer the humiliation of wearing cast-off clothes that were *handed down* from your older brother or sister. And now, as an adult, the humiliation continues, because many of your possessions are **hand-me-ups**. Your mobile phone belonged to your son – he's replaced it with the latest model – and you're wearing a dress of your daughter's – it was simply too 'last year' for her …

'It was a **hand-me-up** from my son, Jim, who turned into a fairly conservative guy and wouldn't wear it anymore.'

(*Standard Net, Utah*, 19th June 2005)

healthspan

/ˈhelθˌspæn/ noun [C]

As you reach for another beer or cigarette, think of your **healthspan**. For those of us who live in the Western world, lifespan is significantly longer than **healthspan** – the period of our lives when we are free from serious illness. Our life expectancy might have increased, but what we need to think about is staying healthy as the wrinkles start to form and our hair turns grey …

'. . . a 10-year plan to end ageism, improve health and social care, and encourage us to modify our lifestyle now to make living longer a pleasurable experience. The lag between **healthspan** and lifespan is serious. None of us look forward to chronic illness.'

(*Guardian*, 13th May 2002)

Hinglish

/ˈhɪŋglɪʃ/ noun [U]

In 21st century English, it seems we're more likely to get our *chuddies* in a twist than our *knickers*. The growing influence of the Indian subcontinent on the English language has given us **Hinglish**, a fashionable mix of English and Hindi which has had such an impact that it's putting words like *Angrez* (English person) and *badmash* (naughty) into the dictionary. Now that's interesting, *innit?*

'First it was Indian cuisine, then Bollywood, followed by Indian fashion. The Indian invasion has reached Britain's vocabulary too. It is now time for some **Hinglish**.'

(*Hindustan Times*, 9th June 2005)

homeshoring

/ˌhəʊmˈʃɔːrɪŋ/ noun [U]

First the business world talked about *offshoring* as employment bases were moved abroad. And now it seems the trend is to move back *home* again, as companies have seen the benefits of locating staff in cheaper rural areas or basing them at home. **Homeshoring** is a cost-effective way of providing an improved level of service from local rather than overseas employees.

'It's not as cheap as offshoring . . . But companies bent on cutting costs also see home agents as a way to avoid some of the consumer complaints common to overseas call centers . . . During the next two years, one of every 10 U.S. call centers is likely to shift at least partly to home-based agents . . . Some dub it **homeshoring**.'

(*Seattle Post Intelligencer*, 9th May 2005)

houseblinging

/ˈhaʊsˌblɪŋɪŋ/ noun [U]

You're driving down a quiet residential street in early December, and are suddenly confronted with a dazzling display. What was yesterday a modest, respectable semi-detached house has in a matter of hours turned into an explosion of electrical activity, a giant, flashing, lighting extravaganza, adorned with Santa, snowman and multitudes of reindeer. This is **houseblinging**, and before you say 'Bah, humbug!' or moan about energy consumption, remember that it's often done for a worthwhile charity.

'Greetings **houseblingers** and their admirers! The new **houseblinging** season is now upon us and we know that many of you have already been preparing furiously for this winter's display . . .'

(*houseblinger.com*, 29th November 2005)

hyperdating also hyper-dating

/ˈhaɪpəˌdeɪtɪŋ/ noun [U]

If you haven't met the partner of your dreams yet, but can't face months or years attempting to find them, why not speed things up and try **hyperdating**? This is the practice of dating lots of different people over a short period of time to check out whether any of them might be right for you. **Hyperdaters** use the Internet to set up as many as ten dates per week, sometimes two or three in one night!

'In our rush-crazed society, where takeout and drive-throughs are commonplace, it's no wonder some of us have come to treat relationships as if they came in to-go bags . . . The people involved . . . have different reasons for **hyper-dating**. But it winds up leaving lots of women, and many men, unfulfilled . . .'

(*Denver Post*, 13th February 2004)

hypnosurgery

/ˌhɪpnəʊˈsɜːdʒəri/ noun [U]

Imagine lying fully conscious on the operating table. The surgeon looks down at you, and as he brandishes his scalpel, you're simply told: 'Relax, you will feel no pain …' It sounds bizarre, but this is exactly the principle behind **hypnosurgery**, where hypnosis is used as an alternative to conventional anaesthesia. The patient stays awake whilst they're operated on and hypnosis allows them to control pain perception. Ouch! – or maybe not, if it works …

'**Hypnosurgery** is being used all over the world and people say they have less post-operative pain and faster recovery.'

(*New Zealand Herald*, 11th April 2006)

ice baby

/ˈaɪs ˌbeɪbi/ noun [C]

Though the expression **ice baby** might conjure up images of the American rapper Vanilla Ice performing his best-known single 'Ice Ice Baby', it has a significant and much more serious meaning in the 21st century. **Ice baby** is the term now given to a baby born from a frozen human egg. As well as assisting women with fertility problems, especially those wanting to protect their fertility prior to cancer treatment, egg freezing could become the ultimate in family planning. Women in their twenties and thirties could delay motherhood by storing their eggs for future use and putting their fertility, quite literally, 'on ice'.

'Egg freezing breakthrough will create generation of **ice babies** . . .'

(*Telegraph*, 9th October 2005)

ICE number

/ˈaɪs ˌnʌmbə/   noun [C]

Most of us carry mobile phones these days, and in times of emergency they are invaluable. But what if you were the victim in the emergency, unable to communicate, but carrying the key to your identity and vital contact information on your mobile? Enter the **ICE number**, where **ICE** stands for *In Case of Emergency*. Add the prefix **ICE** to the name of a relative or friend in your mobile's address book, and a person on the scene will automatically know who should be contacted.

'The growing practice of entering an **ICE number** has been encouraged by emergency responders as an easy, simple-to-implement tool in rapidly identifying and assisting those needing emergency care.'

(*Grand Forks Herald*, 6th August 2005)

infomania

/ɪnfəʊˈmeɪnɪə/ noun [U]

If you regularly send a quick text message while talking to someone, or frequently check your e-mails during your working day, you could be suffering from a new and widespread addiction, potentially more harmful to your concentration than smoking marijuana! Sufferers of **infomania** are distracted from daily tasks because they have the constant urge to read and reply to electronic messages.

'The abuse of "always-on" technology has led to a nationwide state of **infomania** where UK workers are literally addicted to checking email and text messages during meetings, in the evening and at weekends.'

(*999 Today*, 22nd April 2005)

Ingerland

/ɪŋgɜːˈlənd/ noun [U]

For football fans from Penzance to Carlisle, the
Channel tunnel connects France with, not England,
but **In-ger-LAND**. Chanted in the terraces at World
Cup matches, this is the fans' response to the lack of
a melodic third syllable in the word *England*
(/ˈɪŋglənd/), and now has connotations of strongly
patriotic (and sometimes even aggressive) attitudes
to national identity.

'When Spurs went 1—0 up from a pass by a
Dutchman to an Irishman they sang "one nil to
Ingerland", so they also think that Keane is
English too.'

(*Arsenal Times*, 22nd April 2006)

iPad

/'aɪˌpæd/ noun [C]

For the princely sum of £80,000, you too could be the owner of an **iPad**, a cute little residence of approximately 380 square feet and with all the chic of a very popular MP3 player. Aimed at young people hoping to get a foot on the property ladder, **iPads** are smaller than an average one-bedroomed apartment, but bigger than studio flats – which could presumably be described as *iPad nanos*. So what's an *iPad shuffle*? A garden shed perhaps?

'First time buyers frustrated by sky-high house prices will be particularly interested as the builders for the project, Barratt Homes, are proposing almost 300 mini apartment **iPads**.'

(*icWales.co.uk*, 23rd May 2006)

irritainment

/ɪrɪˈteɪnmənt/ noun [U]

We all know those programmes on the TV which we can't quite resist tuning in to each week, even if we know they are trashy and annoying. What about last night's reality TV show? It was rubbish, but you just couldn't stop watching it and everyone was talking about it at lunch today ... These compulsive programmes are irritating but somehow they entertain us – that's **irritainment**!

'Irritainment: Entertainment and media spectacles that are annoying but you find yourself unable to stop watching them. Example: The Jackson Trial; Ben and J-Lo; and so on.'

(*Marshall Democrat News*, 2nd June 2005)

jump the couch

/dʒʌmp ðə ˈkaʊtʃ/ idiom

Are you so in love that you want to leap across pieces of furniture? If so you'd be following the example of actor Tom Cruise as he bounced excitedly across the sofa during a TV interview, and in doing so unwittingly gave birth to a new idiom in the English language. Someone who **jumps the couch** suddenly behaves in such a frenetic way that we're tempted to believe that they've, well, lost it somewhat …

'Wales captain Gareth Thomas "**jumped the couch**" on the BBC following his side's loss to England and of a coach. The only conclusion to be drawn from Alfie's hectic demeanour was that Mike Ruddock left because he had lost the support of his senior players . . .'

(*Planet Rugby*, 21st March 2006)

kidult

/ˈkɪdʌlt/ noun [C], adjective

It's the 21st century and the boundaries between child- and adulthood are disappearing. Kids want to dress and behave like adults. They want spending power and designer gear. Adults are in denial, reluctant to give up the freedom of their youth and still keen on playstations, 'Hello Kitty' handbags, films like *Shrek*, and *Harry Potter* novels. The answer is that we're all **kidults** – not kids, not adults, but people who want the best of both worlds.

'**"Kidults,"** . . . They're well past voting age, but they read graphic novels and collect weird little action figures . . . they have intimate knowledge of *The Simpsons*.'

(*Houston Chronicle*, 15th May 2006)

latte factor

/ˈlɑːteɪ ˌfæktə/ noun [U]

Try cutting out the morning trip to a coffee bar to grab a *latte* on the way to the office, and see how much cash you save. The **latte factor** represents the amount of money we waste each day on quick drinks and snacks. Financial analysts have estimated that if you saved this money each day, you could be a millionaire in forty one years!

'Bach has trademarked the phrase "**The Latte Factor**" to point out to young adults and others that saving $10 a day is no big deal if they factor in how much they spend each day by eating out or by buying a daily latte before they arrive at the office.'

(*StarPhoenix, Canada*, 5th November 2004)

leisure sickness

/ˈleʒə ˌsɪknəs/ noun [U]

You were looking forward to some fun and relaxation over the holidays, so how annoying that you caught a cold and felt totally dreadful. If it's any consolation, so many people regularly have the same experience that psychologists now have a name for it – **leisure sickness** – those illnesses which always seem to occur during weekends and holidays …

'Researchers in the Netherlands say a significant proportion of the population is suffering from so-called **leisure sickness**. They have found 3% of people become ill with a variety of different complaints as soon as they stop working and try to relax.'

(*BBC News*, 24th November 2002)

living apart together also LAT

/ˈlɪvɪŋ əˈpɑːt təˈgeðə/, /læt/ noun [C]

If you'd like to be in a serious relationship, but draw the line at sharing a tube of toothpaste, maybe you should consider becoming a **living apart together**. **Living apart togethers**, or **LATs**, are couples who maintain an intimate relationship but live in separate homes – for a variety of reasons, like children from previous relationships, jobs in different cities, or just because they prefer to have their own front door.

'A social revolution is under way with the emergence of a new form of committed relationship in which couples do everything together while maintaining separate households. An estimated one million couples now fall into this classification, known as Living Apart Together, or LAT . . .'

(*The Times*, 16th December 2005)

living bandage

/ˌlɪvɪŋ ˈbændɪdʒ/ noun [C]

We've all seen the science fiction movies where ailing superheroes undergo a fantastic regeneration, their wounds miraculously disappearing without trace. Although medical advances can't quite make us as indestructible as the characters played by Arnold Schwarzenegger, scientists have now perfected the **living bandage**, a revolutionary treatment which dispenses with conventional bandages and heals wounds through the regeneration of a patient's own skin cells.

'"**Living bandage**" brings revolutionary treatment . . . Thousands of patients with severe burns or long-term wounds that refuse to heal could soon be helped with bandages made from their own skin cells . . .'

(*Scotsman*, 27th April 2004)

man date

/ˈmæn ˌdeɪt/ noun [C]

A walk in the park, a trip to the cinema, lunch in a restaurant or a chat over coffee, all activities that two female friends could happily engage in without so much as raising an eyebrow – so why shouldn't two blokes do the same? A **man date** is a male get-together that doesn't hinge on classically 'male' activities like business, drinking or sport.

'Simply defined a **man date** is two heterosexual men socializing without the crutch of business or sports . . . Taking a walk in the park together is a **man date**; going for a jog is not.'

(*New York Times*, 10th April 2005)

marmalade dropper (British), also muffin choker (American)

/ˈmɑːməleɪd ˌdrɒpə/, /ˈmʌfɪn ˌtʃəʊkə/ noun [C]

Imagine reading something so exciting one morning that you forget what you're doing at the breakfast table. **Marmalade droppers** in the United Kingdom, and **muffin chokers** in the United States, are those pieces of journalism – stories, photographs, and quotations, which are so shocking that they can cause you to end up with jam on your tie or crumbs all down your skirt!

'Ah, how we Brits like a good, old-fashioned, legover saga to read at the breakfast table – what one editor I know calls a "**marmalade dropper**" (it is such a gripping yarn, your knife hovers above the toast as you read the paper aghast, the marmalade slipping off unnoticed).'

(*Week*, 5th December 2004)

marriage lite

/ˌmærɪdʒ ˈlaɪt/ noun [C/U]

How about entering into a legal relationship which will give you all the financial benefits of marriage, but none of the drawbacks, such as the need for a divorce if you want to get out? This is what is now legally referred to as *civil union*, described informally as **marriage lite**. Just like *Coca-Cola Lite*, **marriage lite** doesn't have all the ingredients of the standard product, but feels like 'the real thing'.

'Civil unions would become a sort of **"marriage lite"**. You could enter into them and take advantage of the legal benefits, but then leave them whenever you wanted. No messy divorces . . . No alimony payments. No child support. All the benefits of marriage without any of the hassle.'

(*World Magazine*, 28th February 2004)

me time also me-time

/'miː ˌtaɪm/ noun [U]

If the pressures of daily life are just getting too much for you, then why not indulge in a little **me time**, time to relax and do exactly what *you* enjoy. Whether it's going to the gym, taking a long, hot bath, or sitting down with a cup of coffee and a large slice of chocolate cake, we all need a little **me time** in our lives …

'Are you allocating enough "**me time**" into your day? It is far too easy to get wrapped up in day-to-day tasks and responsibilities, forgetting to take care of yourself. Choose from a variety of practices that can easily be incorporated for a few minutes each day to bring about inner peace and contentment.'

(*About Inc.*, 6th June 2005)

metrosexual

/ˌmetrəʊˈsekʃuəl/ noun [C], adjective

Epitomized by celebrity icons like photogenic footballer David Beckham, this is the era of the **metrosexual**, the heterosexual male who pays careful attention to grooming. **Metrosexual** guys are straight, urban-based and upwardly mobile, but care about fashion, the condition of their skin, indulge in manicure-pedicure sessions and have even been known to pluck their eyebrows – all habits thought previously to be the preserve of the fairer sex.

'A **metrosexual**, according to New York's finest marketing men, is "a guy who is definitely straight, but has embraced the worlds of grooming facials, shopping with women and . . . their feminine side".'

(*Guardian*, 16th July 2003)

microscission

/ˈmaɪkrəʊˌsɪʒn/   noun [U]

It's good news in the early 21st century if you're one of those people who breaks out in a cold sweat at the thought of having an injection – you no longer need to fear the glint of a needle. A revolutionary new technique called **microscission** uses a stream of gas to bombard small areas of the skin and create tiny holes which allow drugs to be absorbed. The sensation allegedly feels like a gentle stream of air against your skin, much less painful than the prick of a needle!

'. . . in the not-too-distant future, apparently, we can expect to have our vaccinations, our anaesthetics and our drugs delivered through a new technique called **microscission**.'

(*Guardian*, 20th April 2004)

middle youth

/ˈmɪdl ˌjuːθ/ noun [U/C], adjective

If you're over thirty years of age with a responsible job and dependant children, but still enjoy a good party or listening to loud rock music, maybe you're in your **middle youth**. **Middle youths** combine all the responsibilities of adulthood with youthful attitudes and interests. They are too old to be called young, but too young to be called *middle*-aged.

'Even Glastonbury — forever branded in the memory of many for its muddy fields — appears to be tilting towards the "**middle youth**" market with £125 weekend tickets and acts such as Paul McCartney, David Bowie and Paul Weller.'

(*Scotsman*, 16th June 2005)

miswant

/mɪsˈwɒnt/ verb [I/T]

If you've always wanted a brand new car but have never been able to afford one, if there is a whole list of things you'd buy 'if only you had the money', then stop **miswanting** and consider whether these things would really make you permanently happy. Psychologists claim that as humans we are programmed to **miswant**: we mistakenly believe that getting a particular thing is the route to future happiness.

'If you are wondering how anyone could ever **miswant** something, consider how wanting is intrinsically tied to predicting. To want something is to predict that when we get it, we will feel good . . . **miswanting** refers to the fact that people sometimes make mistakes about how much they will like something in the future.'

(*Psychological Science Agenda*, Vol. 18, No. 4, April 2004)

mobisode

/ˈməʊbɪsəʊd/ noun [C]

If you just can't wait until the next instalment of
that new television drama, why not bridge the gap
by watching a **mobisode** or two in the intervening
days? Whether you're standing in a queue or sitting
on a train, grab your third-generation mobile
phone and get a bite-size fix of programmes like
Lost, *24* or *Prison Break*. And if you're a *Dr Who*
fanatic, you could snack on a sixty second
Tardisode.

'The makers of hit show 24 are creating a
spin-off series of one-minute dramas designed
to be viewed on mobile phones. The **mobisodes**
will be offered to Vodafone users in the UK
from January, coinciding with the start of the
thriller's fourth season on television . . .'

(*BBC News*, 11th November 2004)

mockumentary also **mocumentary**

/ˌmɒkjʊˈment(ə)ri/ noun [C]

There was a time when documentaries only featured 'real' people, and 'real' people never became celebrities. In the topsy-turvy world of 21st century telly, reality TV shows make celebrities out of 'real' people, and fictional characters are used to make documentaries. It seems we all enjoy watching highly paid actors pretending to be ordinary people just like us, as they're interviewed in a **mockumentary**.

'A Minnesota college student plans to release a series of films on the Internet containing interviews with the "real" Harry Potter, one "Harry Putter." . . . Jeremy Gustafson, who hopes to be a film director, will get his first chance by creating **mockumentaries** of the famous literary and cinematic character.'

(*United Press International*, 5th June 2006)

mouthbreather also mouth-breather, mouth breather

/ˈmaʊθˌbriːðə/ noun [C] mainly American, offensive

For practically every letter of the English language there's a way of insulting someone. Along with 'moron' and 'muppet', a recent addition at the letter 'm' is the term **mouthbreather**, a not-so-endearing expression for a person we consider to be so stupid that we liken their appearance to someone who breathes through their mouth and has their jaw hanging open in a gormless way.

'These **mouthbreathers** cannot offer any new ideas, so instead of trying to compete with conservatives, they're busy with the electronic equivalent of sticking their fingers into their ears and shouting, "LA-LA-LA-LA, NO ONE CAN HEAR YOU!!" as loudly as possible.'

(*The Jawa Report*, 23rd January 2006)

movieoke

/ˌmuːviˈəʊki/   noun [U], adjective

Here is the perfect pastime for the frustrated actor! If you've always wanted a chance to act out scenes from your favourite movies, then cinema's answer to the *karaoke* could make your dreams come true. Stand in front of the **movieoke** screen, and you too could battle it out with Darth Vader in *Star Wars* or bring the hills alive with *The Sound of Music*!

'The opportunity to mouth "You talkin' to me?" from *Taxi Driver* and "Go ahead, punk, make my day" from *Dirty Harry* has long been irresistible. The surprise is that **movieoke**, a twist on the karaoke sing-along craze, has only just arrived.'

(*The Sunday Times*, 1st February 2004)

muffin top

/ˈmʌfɪn ˌtɒp/ noun [C]

Not a sumptuous layer of chocolate icing covering the upper part of a sponge cake, but an unsightly roll of fat that spills over the waist of low-cut jeans. If you're partial to regular portions of fish and chips or one too many cream cakes, consider whether you might be contributing to your own **muffin top**, a new kind of 'spare tyre' that protrudes between hipster trousers and crop tops.

'An unfortunate side effect of wide, brief-style bottoms is that they can be binding and prone to push excess flesh up into a **muffin-top.**'

(*Monterey County Herald*, 29th May 2006)

muggle also **Muggle**

/ˈmʌgl/ noun [C], adjective

Do you sometimes feel a bit of a **muggle**? This word hit the spotlight through the magical world of *Harry Potter*, where it is used to draw a distinction between ordinary mortals and those possessing the powers of wizardry, but has now become accepted into general parlance as a way of describing someone who is unskilled or lacks knowledge in a particular area. It has even magicked its way into the dictionary.

'Raincoast's lawyers went to Canada's supreme court in order to cast a "silencio" spell, known to **Muggles** as a gag order, forbidding anyone from revealing details of the plot before July 16.'

(*Guardian*, 13th July 2005)

mystery worshipper

/ˌmɪst(ə)ri ˈwɜːʃɪpə/ noun [C]

An unfamiliar face is sitting at the other end of the pew during the 10.30 communion service, clutching a writing pad and making copious notes. Is this person so fed up that they're writing a letter or two? Surely the sermon wasn't *that* boring … If you're a regular church-goer and have recently asked yourself questions like these, then you may have seen a **mystery worshipper**, someone who performs an 'undercover' evaluation of a particular church.

'GOD is watching us, so they say, but this weekend roles will reverse as a small band of **mystery worshippers** will sneak into churches all over London . . . to find out how good they actually are . . .'

(*Wanstead & Woodford Guardian*, 26th March 2005)

nicotini

/ˌnɪkəˈtiːni/ noun [C]

If a smoking ban in bars and restaurants is driving
you crazy, why not curb your cravings without
having to step outside by buying a **nicotini**? The
ultimate kind of *alcopop*, **nicotini** is an alcoholic
drink which is laced with nicotine, and even comes
in a range of flavours. Both the word and the drink
are an innovative blend of *nicotine* and *martini*.

'The regular **nicotini** has more bite than a
martini and leaves a noticeable aftertaste in
the throat. The menthol variety contains crème
de menthe and has a cough drop taste, while
the "Black Lung" includes Kahlua and has a
coffee flavor.'

(*South Florida Sentinel*, 30th July 2003)

nouse

/naʊs/ noun [C]

If you've ever worried about the size or shape of your nose, 21st century technology has provided a whole new way of appreciating it, especially for those of us with physical disabilities. Our noses are no longer just for smelling things, but can be used for moving things too in operating a **nouse**, a device which has the same pointing function as a computer *mouse* but is controlled by movements of the *nose*.

'The computer mouse is no longer so mighty. A Canadian engineer has invented a system that enables a computer user to push a cursor across a screen simply by moving his or her nose. He calls his nose-driven mouse a **nouse** . . . His next plan is to adapt the **nouse** for paralyzed patients in hospitals.'

(*Current Science*, 11th February 2005)

obesogenic

/əʊˈbiːsəˈdʒenɪk/ adjective

We drive to work, sit at a desk all day, periodically consume conveniently packaged foods packed with sugar and fats, and drive home again. Exhausted after a long day, we grab a takeaway and then sit down in front of the telly with a bottle of wine and a packet of peanuts. We're probably becoming rather large too, because all these habits are **obesogenic**, likely to cause us to become excessively fat.

'We live in an **obesogenic** environment — a plethora of fast food outlets, reliance on cars, and offers enticing us to eat larger portion sizes all contribute to the problem.'

(*Telegraph*, 8th October 2003)

orthorexia

/ˌɔːθəˈreksiə/ noun [U]

We're all familiar with concerns about healthy eating, but what if our desire to eat healthy foods was so strong it was actually damaging our mental health? This is what happens to sufferers from **orthorexia**, a nervous condition characterized by an extreme obsession with healthy foods. For **orthorexics**, even a simple drink of tap water is potentially harmful, and pure, organic rainwater is the only acceptable alternative.

'An obsession with healthy eating could be dangerous, doctors have warned. So what's it like suffering from **orthorexia**? . . . **Orthorexics** exhibit an over-enthusiasm for pure eating and healthy food.'

(*BBC News*, 29th March 2005)

pescetarian also **pescatarian**

/ˌpeskəˈteəriən/ noun [C], adjective

If you would never dream of sinking your teeth into the flesh of a chicken drumstick, but have absolutely no problem shelling prawns, or brandishing a knife and fork as you look at the vacant expression of a whole trout staring up at you from the plate, then that counts you among the world's **pescetarians**, those who extend their vegetarian diet by eating fish.

'Though I'm a **pescetarian** and she a lover of all meats, we found harmony divvying up paella — in this case, a medley of rice, seafood and rabbit — in one of Madrid's bullfight-themed restaurants.'

(*Arizona Republic*, 8th June 2006)

phat

/fæt/ adjective

If you're wearing a new outfit and someone describes you as looking 'well **phat**', don't be offended. They aren't referring to your waistline. This is not a new spelling variant of an adjective meaning 'overweight' but an informal way of expressing approval. You can use it to express admiration of various qualities, including being fashionable, intelligent, cool or sexy.

'And English footballers, whatever their faults, just happen to be the coolest, hippest and most emphatically **phat**, def, pukka and "for real" footballers in the entire world.'

(*Guardian*, 23rd October 2002)

phish

/fɪʃ/ noun [C], verb [T]

Look out for a **phish** in your e-mail. No, this is not a picture of a trout or salmon, but a message asking you to click on a link to a web page and confirm personal information. This **phish** is bait – if you get hooked by it, you could be conned into giving personal details and therefore allow fraudsters access to your bank or credit card account.

'Every internet user in Britain must have received a **phish** by now. You know the form: hello, this is Barclays . . . and we're just checking (or testing, or upgrading . . .) our security system, so please click on this link and enter your username and password (or card number and PIN . . .)'

(*Guardian*, 3rd June 2004)

plagiarhythm

/ˈpleɪdʒəˌrɪð(ə)m/ noun [U]

Who could honestly say that they haven't at some time been tempted to take someone else's work and use it as if it were their own? In the 21st century, the Internet gives us the opportunity to plagiarize not just words, but music too. We can download lyrics and tunes and incorporate them into our own musical creations – but will our **plagiarhythm** be spotted?

'Unlike the UK, Houston resists the urge to commit **plagiarhythm** . . . What do you call a song that has the vocals of Destiny's Child's "Bootylicious" welded onto the backing track for Nirvana's "Smells Like Teen Spirit"? "Smells Like Teen Booty," of course . . .'

(*Houston Press*, 2nd May 2002)

pluot

/'pluːɒt/ noun [C]

The supermarket shelves are brimming with exotic fruits these days, and we're still inventing new ones. If you like the taste of apricots but are put off by their suede-like skin, a **pluot** could be just the thing to add to your fruit salad. **Pluots** are two-thirds plum and one-third apricot. They resemble plums in appearance, with a smooth, sleek and shiny skin, but have a sweet, intense flavour.

'Take **pluots** (a hybrid of plums and apricots), for example: Thomas suggests using them in a salsa with pineapple, cilantro and chili, or cutting them in half and stuffing them with a mix of blue cheese and cream cheese.'

(*Bryan-College Station Eagle*, 7th June 2006)

podcast

/ˈpɒdˌkɑːst/ noun [C], verb [I/T]

Gone are the days when we have to put up with listening to our favourite radio programme at an inconvenient time. No longer do we have to listen to things we aren't interested in just to 'get to' the bit we might want to hear. It's the 21st century, and this is the age of the **podcast**. We can pick up our MP3 player, simply download the programme we want from the Web, and listen to it whenever, and wherever, the mood takes us!

'Bookmaker William Hill is to launch daily **podcast** service in time for the start of the World Cup with commentary from the likes of former England footballer Rodney Marsh.'

(*Digital Bulletin*, 9th June 2006)

polyamorist

/ˌpɒliˈæmərɪst/ noun [C]

It seems that in the noughties, having just one relationship is not enough. There is nothing 'casual' about the relationships of a **polyamorist**, who has a serious emotional commitment to two (or more!) other people with the full knowledge and consent of all partners involved. You might think that one relationship is complicated enough, but some **polyamorous** relationships even form a 'triangle', where each person in a threesome has a relationship with the other two.

'**Polyamorists** do not limit themselves to one relationship but maintain numerous relationships, straight or gay. A key element is that they are all serious emotional commitments, not just casual sex . . .'

(*Observer*, 13th November 2005)

polypill

/ˈpɒlɪpɪl/ noun [C]

'An apple a day keeps the doctor away ...' or what about a pill? Imagine a pill that could counteract all the negative consequences of 21st century diet and lifestyle. You could exercise less, eat more, and still stay healthy by taking a daily dose of the **polypill**. The **polypill** is a cocktail of aspirin, folic acid and drugs lowering blood pressure and cholesterol, which could potentially give us an extra eleven or twelve years of life free from heart attacks or strokes.

'The "**polypill**" could advance disease prevention in the western world more than any other single medical invention ...'

(*Press Association*, 26th June 2003)

potscaping

/ˈpɒtˌskeɪpɪŋ/ noun [U]

If your garden is a walled piece of concrete or only just big enough to swing the tiniest cat in, why not try transforming it into something fabulous with a bit of **potscaping**? Use ceramic pots, antique watering cans and reclaimed sinks, fill them with flowers, trees and shrubs, and arrange them carefully to create your own outdoor masterpiece.

'Some garden designers are putting containers in clusters all over the yard, a trend known as **potscaping**. Mix colors among pots or mingle pots planted in single shades.'

(*Lansing State Journal*, 12th May 2006)

pre-heritance also **preheritance**

/ˌpriːˈherɪt(ə)ns/   noun [U/C]

It's a bit of a paradox that most of us only pass our assets on to our kids when we die, at a time when they may not need financial support as much as they did earlier in their lives, and when we're not around to enjoy seeing them reap the benefits! If you want to avoid this, and the pitfalls of *inheritance tax*, you could adopt the principle of **pre-heritance**, and release capital to your offspring before you die.

'. . . Pru UK's director of lifetime mortgages said: "Parents are providing more financial help to their children than ever before, regardless of the age of the child, and I expect this **pre-heritance** to be a trend that continues."'

(*Guardian*, 12th June 2006)

prepone

/ˌpriːˈpəʊn/ verb [T]

Are you exhausted from work and just can't wait until your next holiday? Or are you wishing that you could do that difficult task tomorrow, rather than next week, just to get it over with? And why not have a meeting this Tuesday, rather than Thursday – that would make much more sense … If you're asking questions like these, then the useful new word you need at your fingertips is **prepone**, to arrange something for an earlier time.

'Even if states like Maharashtra, Karnataka and Kerala **prepone** the ban from August 15 to July 29 and amend the Marine Fishing Regulation Act, the Goa government needs to be firm because in the end it is a resource that is slowly dwindling.'

(*Herald, Goa*, 13th June 2006)

protire

/prəʊˈtaɪə/ verb [I]

If you're fed up with your job and retirement still seems many years ahead, why not **protire**? Instead of working away at a high pressure job until you've been alive for more than five decades and your hair has turned grey, make plans to **protire** by the age of thirty-five. Drop that fast-track career and opt for something less stressful and more emotionally rewarding.

'Research shows that previously career-minded thirty-somethings are suffering from burn-out and want to quit . . . Disillusioned with their careers, they are choosing to "**protire**" — or drop out of work with a positive, self-improving aim . . .'

(*Scotsman*, 9th September 2003)

quirkyalone

/ˈkwɜːkiəˌləʊn/ noun [C]

You've been single for some time, and you'd really like a partner, but prefer not to date indiscriminately, and certainly can't bring yourself to sift through a huge pool of potential partners on a dating website. You are a **quirkyalone**, someone who just wants the right person to come along at the right time – even if that means waiting.

'**Quirkyalones** are not anti-love and certainly not anti-sex — merely "anti-dull relationships". They would rather spend time hanging out with friends, people with whom they have a real rapport, than endure a bad date.'

(*Observer*, 1st February 2004)

QWERTY (also qwerty) phenomenon

/ˈkwɜːti fənˌɒmɪnən/ noun [U/C]

Funny to think that, as we search for information on the Web and exploit all the wonders of 21st century technology, we're using a keyboard designed in the 19th century! The QWERTY keyboard was designed to avoid the jamming of frequently used keys, and though the keys no longer stick, the keyboard has, even though there may be far more practical layouts. Hence the **QWERTY phenomenon**: the general tendency we have to stick with something familiar despite the potential for far more efficient alternatives.

'Are libraries stuck in the rut of dated and artificial classification systems that don't reflect the way we think, but it would be too expensive to switch, something like the **QWERTY** phenomenon?'

(*Centre for Policy Modelling, Manchester*, 10th June 2005)

rate tart

/ˈreɪt ˌtɑːt/ noun [C]

Playing poker or blackjack isn't the only way you can use cards to make money. With increasing competition across banks and credit card providers, why not become a **rate tart**, and regularly switch your financial allegiances for maximum benefit? You could take advantage of 0 per cent balance transfers and low interest rates for 'new customers', and when you're not 'new' any more, simply change to a new provider.

'According to leading market analysts, **rate tarts** are costing the UK lending industry over one billion pounds a year. This is pretty much the same as saying that **rate tarts** are saving themselves one billion pounds a year . . .'

(*DailyIndia.com*, 8th March 2006)

rawism

/ˈrɔːɪz(ə)m/ noun [U]

If you think that being a vegan represents the ultimate in disciplined eating, then you'd be wrong. Enter **rawism**, the practice of only consuming seeds, nuts and uncooked fruit and vegetables in a fresh, natural state. For the **rawist**, even an innocent baked potato is potentially carcinogenic, squeezed of its nutritional value by being placed in the oven!

'If you're thinking of experimenting with **rawism**, but worried abouot restricting yourself to fruit, vegetables and nuts, think again. There are plenty of recipes available for raw food menus, although most require more work than your standard weeknight supper.'

(The *Coast*, vol. 11 num 37, 19th–26th February 2004)

regifting

/riːˈɡɪftɪŋ/ noun [U]

If you've run out of time and haven't managed to get a gift for someone, have you ever been tempted to wrap up that unwanted present you'd put away in a drawer after your last birthday? Have you, on the other hand, ever opened a present and thought that it looked strangely familiar? If the answer to either of these questions is yes, then you've either been a participant or victim in the practice of **regifting**, the recycling of unwanted presents.

'So, what to do when a gift just isn't you? Exchanging and **regifting** is something that's always been very taboo . . . but more recently, it's become perfectly acceptable.'

(*About, Inc.*, 27th December 2004)

remanufacture

/ˌriːmænjʊˈfæktʃə/ verb [T]

Get the printer repaired? No way, you'd far rather buy a newer model that does twice as much for half the price, and occupies half the space on your desk. We live in a world where throwing away and replacing is the norm, and we don't even wait until things go wrong. Some industries have responded to our wasteful habits by exploring the concept of **remanufacturing**, making new products from the stuff we discard.

'Cartridge City sells **remanufactured** computer cartridges and refilled toner cartridges for copying and facsimile machines . . . The staff will also **remanufacture** empties while customers wait.'

(*Fort Wayne Journal Gazette*, 24th May 2006)

rendition also **renditioning**

/renˈdɪʃn/, /renˈdɪʃnɪŋ/ noun [U]

You'll have heard the word **rendition**, it usually refers to a particular performance of a piece of music or drama. However, a new sense of the same word has recently been born, and it has a much darker context. Under the administration of President Bush, **rendition** refers to the process of capture and extradition of suspected terrorists. It's a highly controversial political issue disguised by a familiar word – the power of euphemism.

'A new report has accused Britain of being among 14 European countries which colluded with the CIA in running secret **rendition** flights for terror suspects.'

(*Telegraph*, 7th June 2006)

retrosexual

/ˌretrəʊˈsekʃuəl/ noun [C], adjective

If you're the sort of guy who's quite happy to fall out of bed and pull on an old T-shirt and jeans, if you wouldn't dream of spending more than a fiver on a haircut, and nothing gives you greater pleasure than to grab your toolkit and get your hands thoroughly covered in grease and dirt, then you qualify for the term **retrosexual**, the antithesis of the *metrosexual*. Are you image-conscious or 'classically' male? **Metro** or **retro**?

'No botox for the **Retrosexual**. No $1,000 haircuts . . . The **Retrosexual** man eats red meat heartily and at times kills it himself.'

(*Washington Dispatch*, 2nd May 2004)

RIF

/rɪf/ verb [T] (usually passive)

If your job isn't going very well at the moment and you're wondering why anyone bothers to pay you, watch your step. In the 19th century you would have been *sacked* or *laid off*, in the 20th century you could have been *made redundant*, and in the 21st century you run the risk of getting **RIFed**. **RIF** is an acronym for <u>r</u>eduction <u>i</u>n (work)<u>f</u>orce, a new euphemism for job loss which joins a host of others, such as 1940's *letting go* and 1980's *downsizing*.

'. . . federal agencies, under orders to eliminate jobs and cut supervisory layers, paid nearly 200,000 feds $25,000 each to take regular or early retirement. Another 30,000 were **RIFed** to meet new lower job targets.'

(*Washington Examiner*, 22nd May 2005)

rumint also RUMINT

/ˈruːmɪnt/ noun [U]

Were the governments of the United Kingdom and the United States badly informed about the case for the war against Iraq? Was President Bush's administration a victim of **rumint**, or *rumour intelligence*, as it accepted the credibility of information on weapons of mass destruction from some rather unreliable sources? **Rumint** is intelligence information based on *rumours*, rather than facts.

'Ray McGovern, a retired C.I.A. analyst . . . says, and others back him up, that the Pentagon took dubious accounts from émigrés close to Ahmad Chalabi and gave these tales credibility they did not deserve. Intelligence analysts . . . refer contemptuously to recent work as "**rumint**," or rumor intelligence.'

(*New York Times*, 30th May 2003)

salad dodger

/ˈsæləd ˌdɒdʒə/ noun [C]

'Healthy eating' is an alien concept to overweight **salad dodgers**, who regularly tuck into red meat, battered fish, lashings of dairy products, and whose idea of 'five a day' corresponds to five portions of chips. And if you're feeling smug – be honest, there's a bit of a **salad dodger** in all of us, especially at Christmas, the perfect opportunity to indulge our **salad-dodging** tendencies!

'Land of the **salad dodgers** . . . The incidence of obesity in the US has more than doubled since the 1960s and, increasingly, touches a younger and younger demographic, according to a study to be released tomorrow.'

(*Sydney Morning Herald*, 18th June 2002)

Sars also **SARS**

/saːz/ noun [U]

An acronym of _severe acute respiratory syndrome_,
Sars is a pneumonia-like disease which sent
shockwaves throughout the world in the early 21st
century. Just like the common cold but potentially
fatal, **Sars** is caused by a virus, is contagious, and
has no cure. The disease is mainly spread by
contact with an infected person, especially through
coughing and sneezing.

'The mystery virus known as **Sars** flew to
Toronto late in February inside the lungs of a
78-year-old woman . . . She died of **severe
acute respiratory syndrome** on 5 March, but
not before infecting four other members of her
family.'

(_Guardian_, 7th April 2003)

saviour sibling

/ˌseɪvjə ˈsɪblɪŋ/ noun [C]

First there were *designer babies*, and now we have **saviour siblings**, children created with a genetic make-up specifically designed to treat the illness of their older brother or sister. Unlike *designer babies*, motivation for the selection of a **saviour sibling**'s genetic characteristics has nothing to do with hair colour or musical ability, but is strictly health-related.

'The era of the so-called **saviour sibling** appeared to have arrived yesterday as doctors applauded the birth of Jamie Whitaker — called into the world to allow his sick older brother Charlie to live . . .'

(*Guardian*, 20th June 2003)

seachanger

/ˈsiːtʃeɪndʒə/ noun [C] Australian

Are you fed up with the pressures of city life? Do you often dream of making a fresh start where the pace of life is more relaxed and your home has a view of the sea or hills? If so, then like millions of Australians you should become a **seachanger**. **Seachangers** are professional people who opt for a change in lifestyle by moving to the seaside or country.

'Lifesavers in Maroochy Shire on Queensland's Sunshine Coast are wearing footprints into the sand rescuing **seachangers** . . . Not only the lifeguards are exhausted — the new arrivals are putting a strain on health care, public transport, and roads and the locals' patience.'

(*Sydney Morning Herald*, 11th October 2004)

security mom

/British sɪˈkjʊərəti ˌmɒm/, /American sɪˈkjʊrəti ˌmɑm/
noun [C]

American presidential elections have a strong tradition of pigeon-holing members of the voting public. Among the most recent of these demographic labels is the **security mom**, an American mother who is particularly concerned about terrorism and security issues. She's the creation of strategists wanting to gather support by convincing poor old US mums that they're continually under threat of an imminent terrorist attack.

'I am what this year's election pollsters call a "**security mom**." I'm married with two young children. I own a gun. And I vote . . . Nothing matters more to me right now than the safety of my home and the survival of my homeland.'

(*USA Today*, 20th July 2004)

self-build

/ˌselfˈbɪld/ noun [C/U], verb [I/T], adjective

If you've always dreamed of a home which has all the convenience of contemporary design, is eco-friendly, but has the outward appearance and character of a 'period' property, then there's only one solution, build it yourself! **Self-build** projects give DIY fanatics the opportunity to move up a gear and create their dream home from a blank canvas, preferably in an exquisite location.

'In doing so they joined the hundreds of thousands of others who have turned away from ready-made houses and instead have homes built to their own tastes and specifications. Around 25,000 people every year embark on **self-build** projects . . .'

(*Guardian*, 20th March 2004)

senior moment

/ˌsiːniə ˈməʊmənt/ noun [C]

If you can't remember where you left your keys and then discover that you are actually holding them, then dismiss this temporary stupidity as a **senior moment**. With the stress and information overload of 21st century life, not just *senior* citizens, but people of all ages are liable to forget things and have **senior** ... now ... what was that phrase we were just talking about?

'There's a lot to think about when you're going on holiday so having the occasional **senior moment** can be forgiven . . . Asked recently where we were staying in London my mind went blank even though I know every single item on our extensive itinerary backwards.'

(*Howick and Pakuranga Times*, 15th June 2006)

set-jetter

/ˈset ˌdʒetə/ noun [C]

If you're finding it hard to decide where you'd like to go on holiday this year, why not take inspiration from your favourite film, book or TV programme? You too could join the ranks of the **set-jetters**, people who go on a holiday to a particular place simply because they've read about it in a book or seen it in a film or TV show. If you're a *Lord-of-the Rings* fan you might take a trip to New Zealand, and Rosslyn chapel in Scotland is the top choice if you've cracked *The Da Vinci Code*.

'Tourist locations are seeing up to a 30 per cent surge in bookings from "**set-jetters**", who like to visit places depicted in films, it was revealed yesterday . . .'

(*Scotsman*, 9th August 2005)

sex up

/ˌseks ˈʌp/ phrasal verb [T]

You've been writing a report but it just doesn't make interesting reading. You could make it more attention-grabbing by embellishing it with one or two shocking facts, and, well … okay … the information might not be *totally* reliable, but it does a great job of **sexing up** what would otherwise have made a great bedtime read for insomniacs …

'"Based on a true story" usually sets off alarm bells in my head as filmmakers often take liberties by **sexing up** the real-life story for the screen. But on this occasion I wish that Hitchcock had thought about dabbing a tad more colour . . .'

(*Sydney Morning Herald*, 8th June 2006)

sheeple

/ʃiːpl/ noun [plural]

The power of 21st century media tricks many of us into following the most fashionable ideas of the moment. If you're one of those people who tends to follow popular trends and bases their opinions on what everyone else is saying, then count yourself among the **sheeple**. A blend of the words *sheep* and *people*, **sheeple** describes people who are easily persuaded and tend to follow what others do.

'Unfortunately, voters succumbed to the bullying tactics of our elected officials . . . These increased taxes will harm the economy and hurt families. Hopefully, voters will remember in the future that it's "We the people" not "We the **sheeple**."'

(*Macon Telegraph*, 22nd June 2005)

shock and awe

/ˌʃɒk ənd ˈɔː/ noun [U], adjective

If you want to convince someone that you're in control and that there's no point in attempting to resist, adopt the principle of **shock and awe**. Psychological dominance, or actual physical bombardment, is the key to stunning your adversaries into realizing that their opponents are unbeatable and that there's no point in putting up a fight …

'Friday night, we sat in our packed up apartment plotting our invasion. "I vote covert operation," Dave said. "We sneak behind the house with a locksmith and hope she won't call the cops." "I disagree," I countered. "I want to take a more **shock and awe** approach. We drive up, kick down the door and move in."'

(*Monster and Critics.com*, 19th June 2006)

shopgrifting

/ˈʃɒpˌɡrɪftɪŋ/ noun [U]

It's a tempting idea: buy the shirt one day, wear it to the party, carefully repackage it the next day, take it back to the shop, get your money back. Result: you wore something new but didn't spend any money! If you've thought of doing this (or maybe you've even done it), then remember this is **shopgrifting**, which sounds frighteningly similar to something which is totally illegal: *shoplifting*.

'**Shopgrifting** . . . To "rent something for free" by purchasing it at a retailer and then returning it within 30 days for a full refund. The swindler takes advantage of the store and its liberal return policies . . .'

(*Larry C. Adams, CPA,* March 2002)

silver goal

/ˌsɪlvə ˈɡəʊl/ noun [C]

So unfair, two teams play their socks off during a
football match, and then struggle through extra
time knowing that as soon as their opponents
score a 'golden' goal, more than ninety minutes of
blood, sweat and tears will have been wasted.
The solution? The **silver goal** – let the chaps play
on properly through extra time without the threat
of defeat in a split second.

'The controversial **silver goal** ruling will be
used for the first time at the Uefa Cup and
Champions League finals next month. The
system replaces the sudden-death golden goal
system that has been in force for the past few
seasons.'

(*Guardian*, 28th April 2003)

SKI-er also ski-er

/'skiːə/ noun [C]

If you feel disgruntled at the prospect of being six feet under whilst your offspring happily whoop it up on the cash and assets you've spent many decades working for, then why not become a **SKI-er**? **SKI-ers**, people who *Spend the Kids' Inheritance*, decide that they'll enjoy retirement to the full by spending their hard-earned cash instead of leaving it all to their children.

'The majority of Britons do not intend to scrimp during retirement so they can leave an inheritance for younger generations, preferring to become **ski-ers** in their old age, research showed today.'

(*Guardian*, 19th July 2005)

slow city

/ˌsləʊ ˈsɪti/ noun [C]

This isn't a place where you can only drive at ten miles per hour, and where people should walk rather than run. A **slow city** is not a 'city' at all, but a small town which strives to maintain a high-quality living environment, protecting 'green' areas and historic buildings, removing eyesores, and prohibiting car alarms and other noise pollution. **Slow cities** don't have a burger bar on every corner, but favour shops and restaurants with fresh local produce and traditional cooking.

'. . . town councillor Andrea Mearns said Mold had many of the things needed to become a **slow city**. These included a strong sense of culture, food shops, cafes and restaurants, a clean environment, a strong agricultural base and scores of artisan food producers.'

(*icWales*, 21st February 2006)

slow food

/ˈsləʊ ˌfuːd/ noun [U/C]

Burgers, pizzas, and fried chicken, prepared *fast* and eaten *fast*. In an age where *fast food* seems to make the world go round, there's a quiet revolution with a snail as its emblem. Followers of the **slow food** movement, the **slow foodies**, take as much time as possible over their food. They cook locally grown food by painstakingly *slow* methods, promote food and agricultural biodiversity and eat as *slowly* as necessary for maximum enjoyment.

'I believe in **slow food**, eating locally and getting the freshest ingredients, so I expected the Japanese oysters to taste better. Oysters that come from 50 kilometers away ought to beat those that have traveled 5,000 kilometers, right? They didn't.'

(*Bloomberg News*, 7th June 2006)

smart clothing

/ˈsmɑːt ˌkləʊðɪŋ/ noun [U]

Imagine wearing underwear that could monitor your body temperature or heart rate, and if there's a problem, effectively call an ambulance! This is the concept of **smart clothing**, clothes which have some kind of 'intelligent' electronic feature in their fabric. No need to worry about feeling hot and sweaty, you could be automatically cooled down and deodorized by your shirt, and how about a dress which gives you a massage?

'People who think **smart clothing** refers to a suit and tie should get back to climbing their personal greasy pole. One project . . . features a coat with LEDs sewn into the cuff. When the wearer waves, the embedded lights flash on and off in synch with the movements of the arm to spell out "TAXI" in large letters'

(*IT Week*, 22nd May 2006)

smirting

/ˈsmɜːtɪŋ/ noun [U]

Smoking might damage your health, but it could do wonders for your love life. If you need to pop outside for a fag because there's a smoking ban, you could indulge in a spot of **smirting** (*smoking* and *flirting*) with a fellow smoker. **Smirting** is far easier than trying to strike up a conversation at a crowded bar. Simply asking someone for a light avoids any introductory awkwardness, and the five-minute lifespan of a ciggie means that you can just go back inside or carry on chatting, depending on how you feel about the other smoker.

'*Smirting* is the practice of flirting over a smoke at pub doorways. A great way to meet people, it's almost worth taking up smoking for.'

(*Living Dublin*, 2005)

snowrafting

/ˈsnəʊˌrɑːftɪŋ/ noun [U]

If you fancy a little fresh air and exhilaration after gorging on Christmas treats, why not take up one of the latest Winter extreme sports: **snowrafting**. Fun for the whole family and not requiring any level of fitness, you all climb into one large rubber dinghy and get propelled down a steep descent of hard-packed snow, travelling at speeds of up to sixty miles per hour. And don't worry – apparently the experience only lasts a few long, terrifying seconds!

'**Snowrafting** is usually called "white fear", and it usually is the first step for those who want to start trying extreme sports.'

(*Eastern Dolomites Tourist Board*, 2006)

sonic branding

/ˌsɒnɪk ˈbrændɪŋ/ noun [U]

Doesn't that car horn jingle always conjure up an image of a little red telephone on wheels? Of course, it's the insurance company *Direct Line*. And you might not know the first thing about computers, but that familiar sequence of four electronic chimes instantly reminds you it's an *Intel*™ processor. A concept as old as the tinny tunes from an ice-cream van, what used to be a *jingle* is now a **sonic brand**, and the association of a particular tune with a particular product is known as **sonic branding**.

'**Sonic branding** conveys a brand's values through voice, music and sound effects. It is the bugle call of the Direct Line telephone. It's the pat of a pocket full of money saved at Asda.'

(*Telegraph*, 29th December 2004)

speed-dating

/ˈspiːd ˌdeɪtɪŋ/ noun [U]

If you're the sort of person who believes that first impressions are always reliable, then your local **speed-dating** event could be your quickest route to romance. No time for awkwardness or social niceties, **speed-daters** have just eight minutes or less to chat to a potential partner before moving on to the next one, allegedly more than enough time to decide whether you've met someone you'd like to spend the rest of your life with …

'. . . British men and women who lack the time to conduct a gentle courtship have a new way to find a partner. Welcome to the world of **speed-dating**, where young singles can meet a prospective partner on a "dating conveyor belt" that allows them three minutes to decide if this is Mr or Ms Right.'

(*Observer*, 26th January 2003)

spim also spIM

/spɪm/ noun [U]

First there was *spam*, unwanted e-mail, and no sooner had we worked out a way of dealing with it than along came **spim**. Spim is similar in design to *spam*, but instead of working through e-mail inboxes, it attacks users through *instant messaging* (*IM*) services, making advertisements and unwanted messages automatically appear when you are connected to the Internet.

'. . . researchers warn that **spim** is growing at about three times the rate of spam, as spammers adapt their toolkit to exploit a rapidly rising number of new instant messaging (IM) users . . . **Spim** is more insidious than spam because messages pop up automatically when a user is logged in, making them harder to ignore.'

(*New Scientist*, 26th March 2004)

spinach cinema

/ˌspɪnɪdʒ ˈsɪnəmə/ noun [U]

You might feel informed, challenged or even downright depressed, but certainly not entertained. You've been watching a film in the new genre of **spinach cinema**, movies which are educational, but not always enjoyable. Just like spinach, not the most exciting vegetable but packed with goodness, **spinach cinema** is good for the soul but not relaxation for the brain.

'Yeah, it's a documentary about Israelis and Palestinians, but it isn't what a friend of mine calls **spinach cinema**. (Good for you and packed with vitamins, but not so super-interesting.)'

(*Salon.com*, 28th April 2005)

spoiler

/ˈspɔɪlə/ noun [C]

It's a disappointing feeling, you're enjoying the suspense of a murder mystery and then suddenly the person sitting next to you lets slip who 'did it' in a loud whisper – they read a **spoiler** last week on the Internet. Prematurely discovering what is going to happen has *spoilt* your enjoyment of the film, so that there seems little point in watching it now.

'. . . while *The Italian Secretary* is an enjoyable if slightly stretched piece of literary ventriloquism, at its heart lies – **spoiler** alert – a presence that remains unexplained: the ghost of the Italian secretary himself, David Rizzio.'

(*Telegraph*, 19th August 2005)

stage-phoning also stage phoning

/ˈsteɪdʒ ˌfəʊnɪŋ/ noun [U]

You'll have met someone who enjoys **stage-phoning**. Their natural habitat is the seat next to you on a bus or train. As you sit quietly, you hear the ringtone of a mobile phone in their pocket. They answer and shuffle around on their seat. Suddenly everyone knows the name of the person who just rang and is treated to one half of a conversation that they aren't remotely interested in. The **stage-phoner** smiles inwardly, knowing that those around are a captive audience.

'He may engage in what researcher Sadie Plant, author of the Motorola report, refers to as **stage-phoning**, in which the caller is effectively performing for innocent bystanders . . . In extreme cases, performance may, in fact, be the entire point of the call.'

(*Chicago Tribune*, 17th July 2002)

stealth tax

/ˈstelθ ˌtæks/ noun [C/U]

Nobody likes the idea of paying tax. It's our hard-earned money, so it seems unfair when the government snatches some of it. One way a government can make itself instantly popular, therefore, is to pretend that it won't take so much of people's cash. But the money has got to come from somewhere … So why not adopt the principle of **stealth tax**, and take it in ways that you think people don't notice?

'Millions of the poorest pensioners will lose hundreds of pounds a year under Government changes to the pension system, say the Tories . . . Opposition MPs say the changes — uncovered in the small print of the Government's recent pensions White Paper — amount to yet another **stealth tax**.'

(*Daily Mail*, 8th June 2006)

Stepford

/British ˈstepˌfəd/, /American ˈstepˌfərd/ adjective

She's the domestic goddess, sweet-natured and subservient, the **Stepford** wife. Her natural extension is the **Stepford** husband, the successful, caring chap who never strays, and **Stepford** children, who lead model lives in complete harmony. And then there's the **Stepford** employee, who always toes the line at work, or **Stepford** parents, who are the perfect role models. Compliant, conformist, irreproachable – also now known as **Stepford**.

'The things they do on television, especially in US sitcoms! Sometimes the teens "take out the trash" without being bribed and actually sit at the table en famille at dinner AND chew the fat with ma and pa. These are, obviously, **Stepford** kids.'

(*Tonight, South Africa*, 1st June 2006)

stress puppy

/'stres ˌpʌpi/ noun [C]

You've got so much to do: a difficult project at work, decorating the spare bedroom, repairing the kids' bikes, shopping for dinner, cooking dinner, chairing the next meeting at the camera club, feeding next door's cat, watering the garden … the list is endless. If you secretly enjoy having a good moan about how under pressure you are, but actually thrive on living a busy, stressful life, then that makes you a **stress puppy**.

'. . . When I applied for this position, it was suggested to me that, historically, this has been a job for **stress puppies** with a reckless disregard for their own mental and physical health.'

(*Trent University Community Magazine*, 2002)

studentification

/ˌstjuːdntɪfɪˈkeɪʃən/ noun [U]

It was once a quiet suburb, with pleasant shops and residential areas inhabited by families and older generations. Now the average age seems to be twenty, and every other shop is a takeaway or cheap off-licence. Larger homes are owned by landlords with multiple tenants. This is **studentification**, the environmental and social changes caused by a large influx of students into a particular area of a town or city.

'Other symptoms of **studentification** range from loud late-night music to higher insurance premiums because students attract burglars, soaring rents and the local shop becoming a takeaway.'

(*Guardian*, 24th January 2006)

Sudoku also **sudoku, Su Doku**

/ˌsuːˈdɒkuː/ noun [C]

You don't need to be a brilliant mathematician or word buff, you can be male or female, eight or eighty, British, French or Japanese ... just about anyone can attempt to do a **Sudoku**, the number placement puzzle consisting of a grid and the digits 1–9. A **Sudoku** in the newspaper is now as familiar as the humble daily crossword – and could possibly even overtake it as the most popular way to while away a few spare minutes.

'British Airways has banned its staff from doing **Sudoku** puzzles, arguing that the Japanese numbers game distracts cabin crew during take-off and landing . . .'

(*Australian*, 31st October 2005)

supersize also **supersized**

/ˈsuːpəˌsaɪz/, /ˈsuːpəˌsaɪzd/ adjective

It all started with a particularly large portion of French fries at a well-known fast-food restaurant. But **supersize** portions of food lead to **supersize** people and **supersize** health problems. **Supersize** people need **supersize** homes, drive **supersize** cars and shop at **supersize** shopping malls. We now live in a society where things are not just large, but excessively large, or **supersize**.

'**Supersize** beds, wheelchairs, hoists and commodes are being installed in Hawke's Bay Hospital, Hastings, to cope with a growing number of obese patients . . .'

(*Hawkes Bay Today, New Zealand*, 16th June 2005)

tankini

/ˌtæŋˈkiːni/ noun [C]

All the modesty of a one-piece swimsuit, but with the convenience of a bikini (you don't have to take the whole thing off every time you want to go to the bathroom!). This is the age of the **tankini**, the new take on women's swimwear where the *tank* is a strappy top extending to somewhere between just above the navel and the top of the hips, and the *-ini* is a bikini-style bottom.

'If you're not a bikini gal, try a **tankini**. When you're choosing one, pay close attention to the "meet and greet," the point on the belly where the top of the suit meets the bottom.'

(*Fort Wayne News Sentinel*, 16th June 2006)

tap up

/ˌtæp ˈʌp/ phrasal verb [T]

There was a time when this phrasal verb had a simple meaning you might have predicted, i.e.: 'to wake someone up by tapping at the door'. However, in the 21st century speak of football moguls, **tapping up** has taken on a whole new meaning. A player is **tapped up** if a rival team manager attempts to recruit him when he is bound by contract to another team. A new take on headhunting, **tap up** sometimes appears in non-sporting contexts too.

'As well as being **tapped up** for jobs in foreign markets, planners who started their careers on the creative side of the business don't generally feel the need or desire to stay in the industry when faced with senior management positions.'

(*Media Bulletin*, 7th July 2006)

technology butler

/ˌtekˈnɒlədʒi ˌbʌtlə/ noun [C]

It's the 21st century and room service goes beyond fresh towels or breakfast in bed. Guests in high-class hotels can now rely on the services of a **technology butler** to attend to their technical needs. Just as the maid service fluffs up pillows and cleans the bathroom, **technology butlers** are on call twenty four hours a day to help with Internet access, personal e-mail, international use of mobile phones, conference calls or voltage conversion … no job too small for the 'cyber' concierge.

'Schloss Hotel im Grunewald . . . As well as the usual delights, the Schloss boasts a **technology butler** — surely enough on its own to distract the boys from Berlin's prodigious club scene.'

(*World Cup 2006, Guardian*, 5th June 2006)

textual harassment

/ˌtekstʃuəl həˈræsmənt/, /ˌtekstʃuəl ˈhærəsmənt/ noun [U]

Text messaging is now an integral part of daily life, but with every new form of communication comes the risk of abuse. As well as harassing someone by speaking down a phone, persistent individuals can now use the new medium of texting to make unpleasant and abusive comments – **textual harassment.** Threatening and abusive text messages are particularly frightening because they are very difficult to avoid or ignore.

'**Textual Harassment.** Text messages are cheap and fun, but they can also be used to insult or abuse people. If you get any abusive or harassing text messages don't think there's nothing you can do about them.'

(*One Life, bbc.co.uk*, 29th June 2006)

third of a pint

/'θɜːd əv ə ˌpaɪnt/ noun [C]

Apparently 21st century women still prefer to drink wine rather than beer. In an attempt to convince them otherwise, beer has now become available in **third of a pint** glasses. Women are allegedly put off by traditional half and full pints, and likely to be keener on sipping from more attractive, long-stemmed glasses which hold a **third of a pint**, affectionately known as *thirds*.

'We all know the problem with beer and women — love the taste, but those big glasses are just way too heavy for our feeble, womanly arms. Thankfully, the British Beer & Pub Association has announced plans to launch a new, elegant "**third of a pint**" glass in an effort to coax us off the chardonnay and malibu and onto ale.'

(*Guardian*, 10th March 2005)

thumb generation

/ˈθʌm ˌdʒenəˈreɪʃn/ noun [U]

A broken thumb could potentially have a major effect on a young person's social life. It would stop them being able to text their friends and prevent them from playing their favourite electronic games. They are members of the **thumb generation**, a generation of young people and adults whose enjoyment of leisure time relies heavily on how quickly their thumbs can press a keypad.

'In the kitchen are Julia Leihener's Thups, drinking glasses which rest on the thumb for the new "**thumb**" **generation** of texters and computer gamers . . .'

(*Art Daily*, 15th June 2005)

tofurkey

/ˌtəʊˈfɜːki/ noun [C/U]

Vegetarian alternatives often bizarrely imitate the
meat products that non-meat eaters are reputedly
trying to avoid. The barbecue or grill is no longer
the preserve of the carnivore, with veggie burgers
and veggie sausages galore. And it now seems that
Christmas is no exception, thanks to the **tofurkey**.
Vegetarians, too, can have a bona fide centrepiece
on the festive table, courtesy of a bird-shaped hunk
of tofu.

'Good News For Vegetarians & Turkeys . . .
Whether you are seeking to offer a meatless
option for a portion of your dinner guests or
are planning a complete vegetarian feast,
tofurkey will satisfy and amaze all who try
it . . .'

(*Turtle Island Foods*, November 2003)

togethering

/ˌtəˈɡeðərɪŋ/ noun [U]

Far from seeing a holiday as an opportunity to 'get away from it all', it seems that some people prefer to go on vacation surrounded by familiar faces. **Togetherers** are folks who like to spend their annual holiday with extended family and friends – one big, happy crowd of parents, kids, siblings, aunts and uncles, nephews and nieces, colleagues from the office or mates from the local club.

'More and more, Americans are vacationing in a loving gang, it seems. This trend toward mob bonding is called "**togethering**" . . .'

(*San Diego Union Tribune*, 29th April 2004)

trolleyology

/ˌtrɒliˈɒlədʒi/ noun [U]

You see somebody really good-looking at the supermarket checkout and then notice that their trolley is full of beer and frozen hamburgers. Suddenly your opinion of them changes – maybe they're too lazy to cook decent food and just spend all their time slumped in front of the TV ...The name for the psychological assessment you have made is **trolleyology**, the study of how the contents of a person's shopping trolley show something about their personality.

'**Trolleyology** is a term concocted by American anthropologists, who claim that your trolley contents not only reveal your personality, they can also speak volumes about your sex drive . . .'

(*Mercury, South Africa*, 29th October 2004)

trout pout

/ˈtraʊt ˌpaʊt/ noun [C]

Anyone contemplating cosmetic surgery to produce beautiful, 'plump' lips should consider the cautionary concept of the **trout pout**. Collagen injections are supposed to give women full, luscious, attractive lips, but it seems that they are just as likely to produce prominent, comically over-sized ones resembling those of a dead fish …

'Society's obsession with high cheekbones and luscious lips has prompted thousands of Britons to resort to implants to enhance their features. Mockingly termed the **trout pout**, a collagen lip injection is one of the most common treatments, which costs as little as £300.'

(*The Times*, 29th January 2005)

truthiness

/'tru:θɪnəs/ noun [U]

The problem with the truth is that it's just not interesting enough. It is also sometimes rather inconvenient. So out with the truth, and in with **truthiness**. Much more appealing are those facts which we'd like to speculate are true, even though we don't know for certain that they are true. The word **truthiness** conveniently places itself somewhere between the actual truth and the conviction of belief or opinion.

'A better word could not have been coined to describe the current debate over global warming . . . The . . . most bizarre example of **truthiness** is that we have a number of cheap, nonpolluting and renewable sources of energy we can exploit.'

(*News-Press, Florida*, 18th January 2006)

tsunami

/ˌ(t)suːˈnɑːmi/ noun [C]

On 26th December 2004, a natural disaster killing over 270,000 people in Asia catapulted a previously unknown word into the everyday speech of millions. Originating from the Japanese words *tsu* ('harbour') and *nami* ('wave'), a **tsunami** is a series of waves generated when seawater is rapidly displaced on a massive scale. Its effects can range from unnoticeable to devastating. We now use the word figuratively to describe a sudden influx or deluge of any kind.

'A hot new social-bookmarking site is deluging web servers all over the net with a **tsunami** of traffic . . .'

(*Wired News*, 17th November 2005)

twixter

/ˈtwɪkstə/ noun [C]

There was a time when reaching the age of twenty-one signalled the onset of adulthood and all its associated privileges and responsibilities – freedom to live how you want, but paying for it yourself. In the 21st century however, it seems that there's an intervening stage of development between adolescence and full-blown adulthood: meet the **twixters**, grown-up offspring in their twenties, who live at home with the safety net of Mum and Dad as financial back-up.

'. . . a "**twixter**", a "parasitic single". I am part of a growing breed of people both in the UK and US who either fly back into the nest, or don't fly out at all.'

(*Guardian*, 5th July 2005)

ubersexual

/uːbəˈsekʃuəl/ noun [C], adjective

If the *metrosexual*, a guy in touch with his feminine side, is not your ideal man, then how about the **ubersexual**? Oozing masculinity, the **ubersexual** male is rugged in appearance, confident, and has an unselfish passion for causes and principles – think *Bono*, lead singer of the rock band *U2*. The **ubersexual** grooms his mind and is passionate about his beliefs, the *metrosexual* grooms his hair and is passionate about himself.

'Stand aside oily womanizers and clueless wimps and make way for the passionate **ubersexual** man of the future . . . **Ubersexuals** are the most attractive (not just physically), most dynamic, and most compelling men of their generations . . .'

(*CanWest News Service*, 17th October 2005)

underload syndrome

/ˈʌndəˌləʊd ˌsɪndrəʊm/ noun [U]

Bored to death, or, quite literally, bored sick. Some of us are apparently so lacking in a stimulating supply of things to do that we become ill. Known as **underload syndrome**, symptoms of this recently identified disorder include headaches, fatigue and recurrent infections. The theory is that a lack of challenging activity can cause the body to stop producing vital hormones and make us more susceptible to infection. Better get busy!

'A lack of stimulation at work can have similar negative effects — known to psychologists as "**underload syndrome**". Studies at the University of Northumbria found that bored people have more days off sick than any other group . . .'

(*The Times*, 2nd February 2003)

unschooling

/ˈʌnˌskuːlɪŋ/ noun [U]

Every child's dream – **unschooling** is 'not school'. This is an approach to education where the emphasis is on the learning process itself, driven by the natural instincts of the learner. The idea is that children learn by experience, with textbooks shifting to real world perspectives. How about studying geometry by making a quilt, or learning the principles of algebra by painting a room? – now that sounds like much more fun!

'The . . . boy is part of a small but growing educational movement called "**unschooling**," which allows children to dictate how and when they learn . . . "Some days they feel like learning a lot, and other days they don't," said Richie's mother, Cindy, who equates **unschooling** to following the natural rhythms of life.'

(*Arizona Republic*, 6th June 2006)

vanity sizing

/ˈvænəti ˈsaɪzɪŋ/ noun [U]

You'd always thought you were a size sixteen, so imagine how pleasantly surprised you are when you try on a pair of trousers, and, though the label clearly states 'size twelve', you can zip them up without breathing in and sit down comfortably? Before you get too excited about how you've unexpectedly lost weight, consider the concept of **vanity sizing**, where a smaller-size label is placed on a larger-size garment, specifically in order to please the buyer.

'On the other hand, some clothing companies are using "**vanity sizing**" in a bid to appeal to, for instance, a size 14 woman with a size 8 label.'

(*Globe and Mail, Canada*, 28th June 2006)

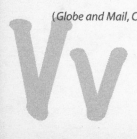

virtual Friday

/ˌvɜːtʃʊəl ˈfraɪdeɪ/ noun [C/U]

A public holiday on Friday this week – fantastic, it's always a great feeling when we know that the working week ahead of us is shorter than normal. A day earlier than usual we begin to anticipate the excitement of the weekend, so that on Thursday we get that slightly relaxed 'Friday feeling', knowing that it's not long before we get a break. This is a Thursday which really feels like a Friday, so why not call it **virtual Friday**?

'Yeah, I know it's only Wednesday but for me it's **virtual Friday**, since I'm off work the next two days and will be offline for the most part.'

(*Personal weblog*, 26th November 2003)

vlog

/vlɒg/ noun [C], verb [I/T]

People who enjoy using a *blog* (weblog) to write
endlessly about everything that matters to them in
life, whether it's politics, global warming, computer
software or the weekly rubbish collection, can now
take their web-based commentary to the next level.
'Pictures speak louder than words', it seems, as
many ardent *bloggers* are now becoming **vloggers**
– filming and broadcasting their ideas in a *video
blog*, or **vlog**.

'As with other parts of the Internet, the
topics for **vloggers** are as diverse as the
people who **vlog** – from cooking lessons or
political protests to a single dad showing how
to change a diaper . . .'

(*Lexington Herald-Leader*, 15th October 2005)

vodcast

/ˈvɒdˌkɑːst/   noun [C], verb [I/T]

Technology never stands still. Just when we'd got to grips with the idea of a *podcast*, a downloadable audio programme, along came the video-enabled iPod, capable of playing video material on a miniature screen. So now it's not just audio, but also video, which can be grabbed from the Internet and squeezed onto a portable device, and along with *podcasts* we have **vodcasts**, revolutionizing the world of TV and video by allowing viewers to download and watch the programmes of their choice.

'In an exclusive Times **vodcast** to mark the opening of a new exhibition at the Gagosian Gallery, in West London, Damien Hirst also reveals that future work may involve a crucifixion.'

(*The Times*, 1st July 2006)

voice lift

/ˈvɔɪs ˌlɪft/ noun [C]

A woman might have kept her youthful looks, or paid a lot of money for a face lift. But as soon as she begins to speak, that croaky old voice is a giveaway: she must be over sixty ... People who want to disguise their age through their voice as well as their looks can now buy a **voice lift**, and have surgery on their vocal cords to make them sound younger.

'. . . The latest luxury for aging baby boomers looking for the fountain of youth is the so-called "**voice lift**", designed to make patients' voices sound more youthful.'

(*ABC News*, 22nd April 2004)

voluntourism

/ˌvɒlənˈtʊərɪz(ə)m/ noun [U]

If you fancy going on a holiday, not just 'with a difference', but which 'makes a difference', then you should know about the new trend of **voluntourism**. **Voluntourists** head to far-flung parts of the world, not just to soak up the sun and see the sights, but to build walls, dig fields, and clean out baboons and elephants. They rebuild by day, and party by night.

'The effort is dubbed **voluntourism**, and local leaders say it is critical to the rebuilding because it provides dollar-spending fun lovers and hammer-wielding fixer-uppers all rolled into one . . .'

(*Washington Post*, 15th March 2006)

VoIP also **voip, Voip**

/vɔɪp/ verb [I/T]

It's good to talk. If certain members of your family enjoy regular, hour-long chats on the phone with friends all over the world, and this has a rather agonizing effect on your phone bill, then maybe it's time you embraced 21st century technology and thought about **VoIPing** – or in other words, making telephone calls over the Internet. **VoIPing** can be cheaper than conventional or mobile telephone services, and is sometimes even free – now it really does seem good to talk ...

'If you're sick of being charged over-the-odds prices for making calls abroad on your mobile, it's probably time you **Voiped**.'

(*Guardian*, 26th May 2005)

WAG also Wag

/wæg/ [C]

Football is sometimes described as a 'game of two halves', but what about the *other* halves? **WAG** is an acronym of *wife **a**nd **g**irlfriend*, and refers to the female partners of famous professional footballers. Whilst their menfolk run feverishly around the pitch shouldering the aspirations of football supporters across the globe, the **WAGs** have a reputation for designer shopping by day, and partying by night.

'Until now, it was reckoned that the **Wags** had a more successful World Cup than the lads. Tales of players' wives spending £57,000 in an hour's designer shopping or dancing on table tops after running up £400 cocktail bills overshadowed the team's pedestrian outings on the pitch.'

(*Guardian*, 10th July 2006)

walking bus

/ˈwɔːkɪŋ ˌbʌs/ noun [C]

If, on the way to work in the morning, you regularly come across an orderly group of walking children flanked by adults in fluorescent tabards, then you'll have seen a **walking bus**. In an effort to encourage walking as a healthy and environmentally friendly option, a **walking bus** is a group of kids who walk to and from school supervised by two or more adults, usually with a 'driver' at the front and a 'conductor' bringing up the rear.

'. . . ethical initiatives . . . begin before the first bell, when the **walking bus** sets off, gathering pupils and trotting along emission-free to the school gate.'

(*Observer Magazine*, 18th June 2006)

warchalking

/ˈwɔːtʃɔːkɪŋ/ noun [U]

In the noughties, not all the symbols you see
scrawled on public pavements and buildings are
mindless graffiti. If you've been walking to the
office and noticed an increasing number of chalked
or spray-painted symbols resembling those in a
game of noughts and crosses, then you've probably
seen evidence of **warchalking** – a way of
indicating to people where they can take a
wireless-enabled laptop and go online – for free.

'Phone maker Nokia has come down strongly
against **warchalking**. It has condemned as theft
the placing of chalk symbols on walls and
pavements at places where people can use
wireless net access.'

(*BBC News*, 19th September 2002)

wardrobe malfunction

/ˈwɔːdrəʊb mælˈfʌŋkʃn/ noun [C]

The next time you have that awkward situation of discovering that your jeans zip is undone in public, you could disguise your embarrassment by apologizing for a **wardrobe malfunction**.
A **wardobe malfunction** is a situation where a person, especially a celebrity or someone in the public eye, accidentally exposes a part of their body because of some kind of problem with what they are wearing.

'Tara Reid says she had no idea she was flashing the paparazzi when the strap of her dress slipped off her left shoulder . . . The 29-year-old actress said she was upset at the photographers' reaction to her **wardrobe malfunction**.'

(*Chicago Sun-Times*, 22nd January 2005)

WiFi also **Wi-Fi, Wifi, Wi-fi, wifi**

/'waɪfaɪ/ noun [U]

It might sound prehistoric, but believe it or not there was a time when, in order to use the Internet or access your e-mail, you had to be strategically positioned inside a building within so many feet of a telephone cable. Today, by contrast, you can sit in a café, lie on the beach, soak in the bath, climb Everest, or be just about anywhere – and still surf the net to your heart's content. This is all made possible by the wonders of **WiFi** (*Wireless Fidelity*), a networking system which provides wireless connection to the web.

'At the moment, nothing says "wired" quite like "wireless", so Paris plans on blanketing the city with a free **WiFi** network operated by private companies.'

(*Ars Technica*, 5th July 2006)

wiki also Wiki

/'wɪki/ noun [C]

You might only know one or two things about growing tomatoes. But if Internet users across the globe share their tomato-growing experiences, the result is a great big repository of tomato horticulture. Harnessing the global knowledge of web users is now made possible through the **wiki**, a web page which you can read, add to and edit, and thereby contribute to what represents the biggest encyclopaedia the world has ever known ...

'. . . there are now **wikis** — websites that anyone can edit — on everything from Tolkien to travel . . .'

(*Guardian*, 1st April 2004)

Winterval

/'wɪntəvl/ noun [C/U]

This festive season, you'll no doubt be sending
Winterval cards, decorating your **Winterval** tree
and tucking into **Winterval** pudding and
Winterval cake. If all this sounds a bit odd, consider
that the word *Christmas* is rather biased towards
one particular faith. In an effort to embrace all
religions, not just Christianity, during the festive
season, the term **Winterval** has been suggested as
a politically correct alternative.

'. . . time for Australia to fall in line with
places such as the UK, where councils have
renamed Christmas "**Winterval**" and replaced
references to Christmas on signage with the
words "Festive" and "Winter".'

(*Queensland Sunday Mail*, 4th December 2005)

xenotransplantation

/ˌzenətrænsplɑːnˈteɪʃn/ noun [U/C]

It's a serious and global problem – the shortage of donor organs for people with life-threatening medical conditions. In an effort to address it, medical science is now exploring unconventional resources: if human organs aren't available, why not use animal organs to save lives? This is the concept of **xenotransplantation**, the surgical transfer of cells, tissues or whole organs from one species to another.

'**Xenotransplantation** would provide a vast and instantly available army of potential donors, with pigs the favoured candidates.'

(*Belfast Telegraph*, 26th June 2006)

yottabyte

/'jɒtəˌbaɪt/ noun [C]

Most people will have heard of a *kilobyte*, *megabyte*, or *gigabyte*, but they're all small beer compared to a **yottabyte**. This is a unit of computer storage which represents something like 10^{24} bytes, or, more precisely, 1,208,925,819,614,629,174,706,176 bytes. Commonly abbreviated to *YB*, the **yottabyte** is the largest unit of measurement for computer data. A **yottabyte** really is a 'lotta' bytes!

'In ten years, the volume of online data accessible either on the Internet or on corporate networks is expected to approach a **yottabyte** . . .'

(*Business Wire*, 27th October 2000)

yummy mummy

/ˈjʌmi ˌmʌmi/ noun [C]

Most of us who have experienced the joys of motherhood will probably feel the term 'slummy mummy' is more appropriate, as we look at our waistline and the state of our wardrobe, but wouldn't it be great to be a **yummy mummy**? **Yummy mummies** are immaculate in appearance with a wardrobe to die for, and have sylph-like figures mysteriously unaffected by the rigours of childbirth.

'Actress Kate Winslet has been voted Britain's top **yummy mummy**. The *Titanic* star beat Victoria Beckham and Gwyneth Paltrow in a poll of gorgeous mums.'

(*Daily Mail*, 4th September 2005)

zombie

/ˈzɒmbi/ noun [C]

Could there be a **zombie** lurking somewhere around your home? No, this isn't a lazy teenager or even a dead person brought to life by witchcraft, but a personal computer sitting innocently in a study or living room. Without the owner's knowledge, a **zombie** computer has been affected by a virus and is continually sending out large amounts of spam.

'One alarming trend to emerge from the survey was the increasing number of **zombie** computers — PCs that have been compromised remotely by hackers or virus writers . . . **Zombie** computers are sending out over 40% of the world's spam, usually to the complete ignorance of the PC's owner.'

(*ITWeb, Johannesburg*, 5th January 2005)

zorbing

/ˈzɔːbɪŋ/ noun [U]

If bungee-jumping just seems like yesterday's news, why not grab that adrenaline rush by trying one of the world's latest extreme sports, **zorbing**. Participants are strapped inside a giant plastic ball, with no brakes and no steering, and launched off a hillside, or for more adventurous **zorbonauts**, a cliff or waterfall. They can even opt for a **wet zorb**, and have the ball filled with water. **Zorbing** doesn't require any level of skill or fitness, just the ability to keep down your food!

'If you're a fan of topsy-turvy thrills and the thought of bounding down a grassy hill inside an enormous beach ball doesn't worry you, then **zorbing** is a fantastic experience . . .'

(*BBC Dorset*, 26th April 2006)